MILNER CRAFT SERIES

Netted Lace

Exquisite Patterns and Practical Techniques

Margaret Morgan

SALLYMILNER PUBLISHING

First published in 2014 by
Sally Milner Publishing Pty Ltd
734 Woodville Road
Binda NSW 2583 AUSTRALIA

© Margaret Morgan 2014

Design: Anna Warren, Warren Ventures Pty Ltd
Editing: Anne Savage

Printed in China

National Library of Australia Cataloguing-in-Publication entry

Author:	Morgan, Margaret, author.
Title:	Netted lace : exquisite patterns & practical techniques / Margaret Morgan.
ISBN:	9781863514514 (paperback)
Series:	Milner craft series.
Notes:	Includes bibliographical references.
Subjects:	Lace and lace making. Lace and lace making--Patterns. Lace craft.
Dewey Number:	746.22

Disclaimer
Information and instructions given in this book are presented in good faith, but no warranty is given nor results guaranteed, nor is freedom from any patent to be inferred. As we have no control over physical conditions surrounding application of information herein contained in this book, the author and publisher disclaim any liability for untoward results.

10 9 8 7 6 5 4 3 2 1

Contents

Acknowledgements

I would like to thank Arrienne Wynen, who proofread the draft of the manuscript for me and tried out some of the patterns.
My thanks go also to Maria van Gangelen, who made the bag for Rings of Fire and stitched the lace to it. I would especially like to thank my husband, John, who has always supported me in all my endeavours, even to the extent of having a go at netting.

Introduction

Netting has its origins in prehistoric times with the invention of fishing nets. At some stage this practical craft was extended to decorative purposes, and used to adorn clothing and other household items. The exact history of this development is uncertain, but what is clear is that netting has a very long history and is one of the very earliest forms of lacemaking.

Although I have always been interested in history, it was not its history which initially enticed me to try my hand at netting. My introduction came via filet lace. I had been making filet lace for a couple of years, quite happily using machine-made net, but then I decided I should try working filet the traditional way on a hand-knotted net. Having no one to show me the technique, I managed to learn it from books, and so I made my first (not very good) piece of traditional filet lace. After that, I made samples of net using different gauges to determine what size meshes they would produce. I realised that being able to make my own net meant I was no longer restricted to the sizes of the commercially made nets. It would also mean that I was not restricted to the colours of those nets, but could make any colour net that I chose.

Thus, my first interest in netting was how it could improve my filet, but I soon started reading old books and magazines in which I saw examples of circular netting. Circular netting, I thought, had great potential for miniatures. Then I realised that the variety of different stitches would make beautiful full-size scarves. By this time I was hooked and was just enjoying experimenting. I hope that this book will capture your imagination and that you too will enjoy experimenting with netting.

Section 1
Techniques

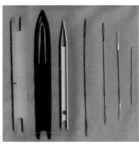
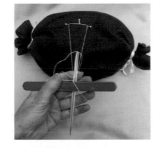
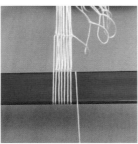

CHAPTER 1
Equipment

As netting is an old technique which has been out of favour in recent years, netting tools are not to be found in all needlework shops. However, do not let that deter you, as the equipment can be bought by mail order from specialist lace shops. Your local Lace Guild should be able to put you in touch with these suppliers. Alternatively, you can search for netting needles and mesh sticks in second-hand shops, especially at those that have a good collection of needlework tools. Or you can improvise and make your own needle, and use things such as tongue depressors as mesh sticks to get you started. 'Where there is a will there is a way.'

The netting knot might at first look difficult when you read written instructions and try to follow diagrams, but in reality it is quite simple and once mastered, it is only a matter of repeating that same knot in order to produce beautiful lace items. As it is an addictive craft, like so many other crafts, you need to be careful to take precautions to protect your wellbeing. A few simple tips are: make sure that your pillow is at a comfortable height for working, so that you are not constantly bending over your work; always work in good light; do not work for hours at a time without a break.

Netting needles and shuttles

The purpose of netting needles and shuttles is simply to hold the thread. They do not determine the size of the meshes of the net (it is the mesh sticks that do this). But of course, you cannot work with a thick thread on a small needle. Consequently, netting needles and shuttles come in many different shapes and sizes. There are large plastic shuttles which resemble the much bigger ones that fishermen once used for making fishing nets and that were used during the Second World War years for making camouflage nets. Large shuttles, like the black and cream plastic ones in the photograph, are convenient for making items such as scarves, which may be netted with wool or other bulky threads.

When it comes to making lace and using fine threads, however, a steel netting needle is preferable. These steel needles also come in different sizes, and you can choose a size to suit your thread. If you venture into miniature netting, then even the finest netting needle is too large to go through the small loops. For miniature netting I use a long needle called a reweaving or filet needle. This is a long needle with a knob on the end that is also invaluable for working the embroidery stitches of filet lace. It is available from suppliers of lace-making equipment. For miniature netting I use this needle, threaded with as long a thread as I can conveniently manage.

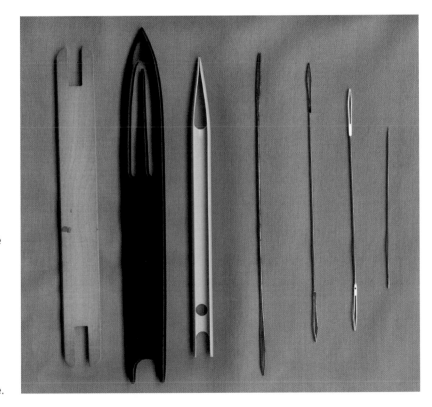

Netting needles. From left to right: hand-made wooden needle, two different kinds of plastic shuttles, three different sized metal needles, and a filet needle.

Mesh sticks and double-pointed knitting needles

Mesh sticks also come in a variety of sizes. The mesh stick determines the size of your loops, and so you need a number of different sizes in order to work interesting patterns. Sets of mesh sticks can also be bought from suppliers of lace-making equipment, but you can sometimes pick them up in second-hand shops as well. Modern mesh sticks are usually made from plastic, but old mesh sticks were made from wood, bone or even ivory. The size of the mesh stick is determined by its width. Where a pattern in this book calls for a 6 mm mesh stick, for example, it means a mesh stick that is 6 mm wide. The pattern for the scarf with long loop centre and short loop border (page 63) even calls for a mesh stick 39 mm wide. I improvised here with a plastic ruler.

As well as mesh sticks you will need a range of sizes of steel double-pointed knitting needles. These knitting needles are used instead of mesh sticks when you are working small loops.

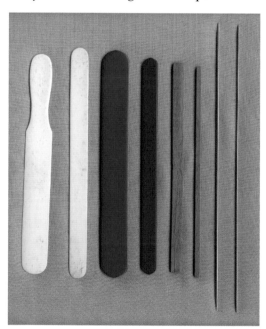

Mesh sticks. From left to right: two old bone mesh sticks, two modern plastic sticks, two wooden sticks, two steel double-pointed knitting needles.

Pillow

In order to make net you need something to anchor it. It needs to be heavy or strong enough so that it does not move when you pull on the net to tighten your knots. You can use a G-clamp for this purpose, and I have read that in the old days people used to use their outstretched foot as an anchor for their netting. This, I think, would become very tiring. I find that a pillow is the most convenient and versatile anchor. The pillow needs to be filled with something to make it heavy. Some people use a 2 kg bag of rice, but I use a pillow filled with propagating sand purchased from a nursery centre.

How to make a sandbag pillow

Fill a plastic bread-bag with approximately 2.5 kg of clean dry sand. Put this inside another bread-bag for extra strength, and tie the end so that it forms a thick sausage shape. Put this inside a section of nylon stocking and knot the ends. Finally, put the pillow inside a fabric cover and tie the ends with ribbons. You can make the fabric cover yourself, and it is best to use a plain dark colour so that, when working with fine light-coloured thread, it is easy to see the net against the dark background of the pillow.

Pins

Glass-headed pins are used to attach the foundation loop of the netting to the pillow. The foundation loop is simply a length of thread with the two ends knotted together to form a circle. To start netting you tie your thread from the netting needle to the foundation loop and then begin making knots on the foundation loop, using a mesh stick to regulate the size of the netted loops.

Pillow with foundation thread looped around pins, and a piece of circular netting begun.

CHAPTER 2
Basic knots and simple netting

The knot generally used for netting is the fisherman's knot, although other knots can be used and are sometimes shown in netting books (see, for example, *The Art of Netting*, eds J. & K. Kliot). Even with this single knot, there is more than one way of working it. Two methods are shown below. The first method is the one most often illustrated in old books on netting, and is the one that I learnt first. The second I learnt at a filet lace workshop in Finland, and is the method I use when working miniatures, as it is especially good when you are using a long needle rather than a netting needle. Both methods give exactly the same result, that is, the finished knot is exactly the same. It is only the way of manipulating the thread that is different. It is a good idea to try both methods to see which you prefer.

The instructions assume right-handedness; if you are a leftie you will need to reverse the way of going.

Basic knot: method 1

Step 1

Make a foundation loop and pin it to the pillow. Wind some thread onto a netting needle and knot the end of the thread to the foundation loop.

Hold the mesh stick in the left hand as shown in the diagrams in this chapter. Bring the working thread (that is, the thread coming from the netting needle) in front of the mesh stick, around the third and fourth fingers of the hand, behind the mesh stick, and then over towards the left, holding it in position with your thumb, and back again towards the right.

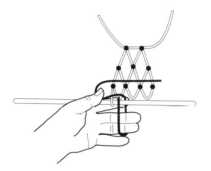

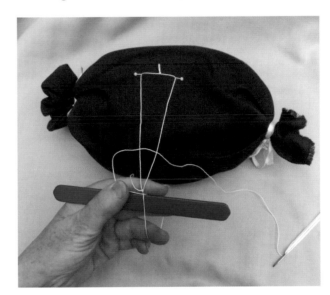

Diagram 1 The working thread is shown in black. This diagram, and diagrams 2, 3, 5 and 6 show some rows already worked and a knot being made into the second loop of a new row (the first knot of the row has already been worked).

This photograph, and the photographs on pages 16 and 17, show the knot being worked into the foundation thread to make the first row.

Step 2

Take the thread behind the mesh stick, behind your fingers, making sure that the thread loops around your little finger (see diagram 2). The netting needle now passes behind the mesh stick and up through the loop formed around the third and fourth finger, and then up through the loop of the previous row of net (or through the foundation loop for the first row), and finally in front of the thread being held by the thumb.

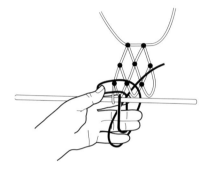

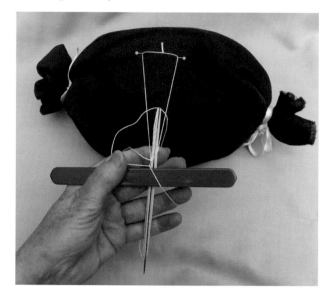

Diagram 2 Bringing the needle up through the loops.

Step 3

To pull the knot tight, proceed as follows: release the thread being held down by the thumb. Slip the third and fourth fingers out of the loop surrounding them, but with your little finger keep hold of the thread which loops around it. It is the little finger which regulates the tension. Make sure that your index finger is not caught up in the loop. Gradually pull the netting needle upwards, away from you, until the knot to be formed is sitting in the correct position at the top of the mesh stick. This can be held lightly in place by the index finger. Now pull the netting needle down towards you, at the same time removing your little finger from the loop, until the knot is tight. It works best if this operation is done in a smooth, not jerky, fashion.

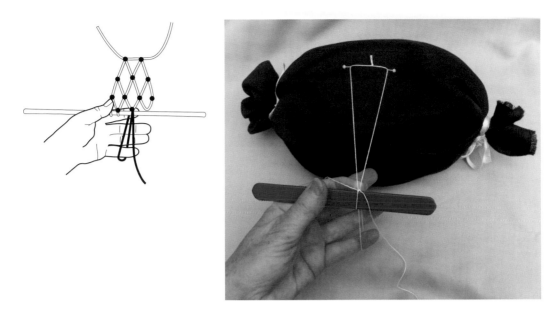

Diagram 3 Ready to pull the knot tight. The index finger is holding the knot in position and the little finger is tensioning the thread.

Diagram 4 shows the route of the thread without showing the fingers. The shaded thread represents the previous rows of net. The unshaded thread is the working thread. The mesh stick is here drawn lower than it should be, so that the direction of the thread can be seen more clearly. Normally the knots sit right on top of the mesh stick (see the photograph with diagram 3).

Diagram 4

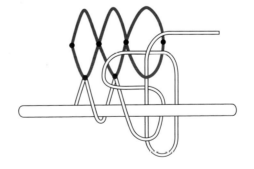

Basic knot: method 2

Step 1

Knot the working thread to the foundation loop. Take the thread in front of the mesh stick, around the fingers (for this method it can go around the little finger as well as the third and fourth fingers) and behind the mesh stick. Take the thread to the left and hold it down with your thumb. Now take the thread over to the right in front of the foundation loop (or previous rows of netting once you have progressed past the first row).

Diagram 5 This first step is the same as the first step for method 1, except that here the thread is going around the little finger as well as the third and fourth fingers.

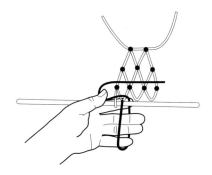

Step 2

Take your netting needle behind the mesh stick and leaving a large loop hanging (this is the second loop), bring it up through the loop which is around your fingers (i.e. the first loop) and up through the foundation loop (or loop of previous row, as in diagram 6a). Diagram 6b shows the route of the thread to this stage.

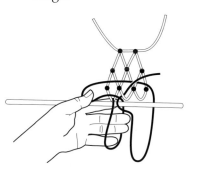
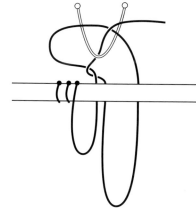

Diagram 6 Bringing the needle up through the first loop and the loop of the previous row.

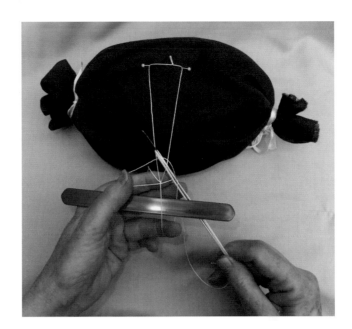

Step 3

Now tighten the knot as follows. Pull the working thread up, away from you, and as you do so remove your fingers from the first loop and place them in the second loop. For this method it is the fingers in the second loop which control the tension. Keep pulling the thread up until the first loop disappears and a knot is formed at the top of the mesh stick. Now bring the thread towards you (see diagram 7). Remove your fingers from the second loop and pull the thread towards you until the second loop disappears and the knot at the top of the mesh stick is secure.

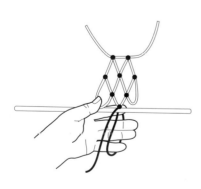

Diagram 7 Ready to pull the knot tight.

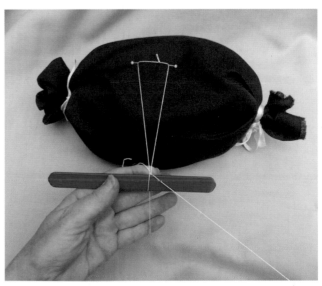

Diamond netting

In order to make a good piece of net it is necessary to practise the basic knot until you are proficient. The best way to practise is to make a piece of diamond netting.

Sample of diamond netting

Make a foundation loop and pin it to your pillow. Wind thread onto your netting needle. Choose a mesh stick of medium size (not too small and not too large). Tie your thread to the foundation loop and then using the mesh stick net 10 loops into the foundation loop. Slide the loops you have just made off the mesh stick. Take the foundation thread off the pins, turn it around and place it back on the pins, so that the working thread is now to the left. Each row is worked from left to right. Again using the mesh stick, make another row of knots, one knot into each loop of the previous row. Slide this row of loops off the mesh stick. Turn your work and net another row. Continue in this way until you are confident that you have mastered the knot. Once you have worked a few rows it is not necessary to take the foundation loop off the pins when you turn your work; you can simply turn the piece of netting so that the working thread is on the left for the start of each row. However, I find it best to turn the foundation thread at the end of each row for the first few rows, as the net sits flatter, without twisting.

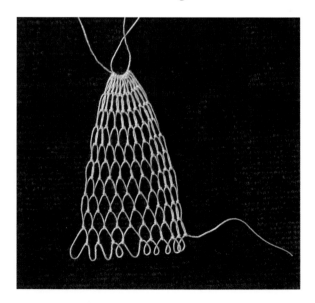

Diamond netting.

Foundation chain

If you are making a large piece of diamond netting it can
be difficult to work with a lot of loops on a foundation loop
(especially if the loops are small), and so it is useful to have a
foundation chain. A foundation chain is simply a long strip of
netting 2 stitches wide. Cast on 2 loops on a foundation loop and
then work a number of rows until you have the required number
of loops down one side. (The size of the meshes does not matter,
as the foundation chain will later be removed, so you can use a
larger mesh stick than the one you intend using for the project.)
Cut off the foundation thread and weave a new thread through
the loops down one side of the piece of netting. Knot the ends
together so that this becomes the new foundation loop, which
you attach to your pillow. The piece of netting is the foundation
chain.

You use the loops which are now on the bottom of the
chain to net into in order to make your project. When you have
finished your piece of diamond netting the foundation chain
can be removed by carefully cutting it away from the rest of the
net. It is a good idea to use a different colour for the foundation
chain so that you do not cut the wrong threads. However, if your
finished article is white, it is best not to use a dark thread for the
foundation chain in case it leaves a mark on the white loops. Pale
blue is a good choice.

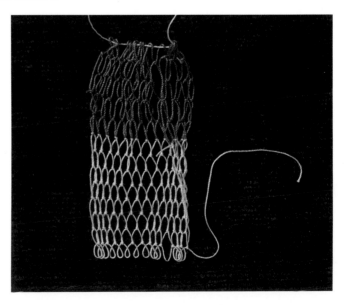

Diamond netting worked
on a foundation chain (pink
thread).

Square netting

The only difference between square netting and diamond netting is that instead of starting with several loops on your foundation thread, you start with 2 loops, and increase 1 loop at the end of each row until you have the desired width. Then you gradually decrease until you are back to 2 loops, which you join together. When you block the piece of net you have a square of net with square meshes. This type of net can be used for filet lace embroidery. Before machine-made net became readily available, the net for filet lace was made by hand in this way, but these days most people use machine-made net. The disadvantage of this is that you are limited by the sizes and colours of the nets that are available. If you make your own you can choose the size of the mesh and the colour of the net, and you can make it in whatever thread you wish – cotton, silk, wool or synthetic yarns.

Here are samples of filet pictures embroidered on hand-made net, where the colour of the net was chosen to blend in with the background so that the net itself is not very visible. This makes the embroidery stand out more.

Filet worked on coloured net. See Appendix 1 for filet patterns.

Sample of square netting

Wind some thread onto a netting needle. Tie your thread to the foundation loop. Choose a mesh stick; one that is neither very large nor very small is best when you are learning. Once you are proficient at forming the knots, you can experiment with different sizes, and if you wish to make a fine net you can substitute a double-pointed knitting needle for the mesh stick.

1st row:	make 2 loops (there will be 3 knots on the foundation loop – the original knot which joined the thread in and the 2 netting knots). Remove the mesh stick and turn the work.
2nd row:	make 1 netting knot into the first loop and 2 netting knots into the second loop [3 loops formed].
3rd and subsequent rows:	make 1 knot into each loop of the previous row and 2 knots into the last loop. By making 2 knots into the last loop of each row the width of the net will gradually increase. Continue in this way until the loops number one more than the number required for each side of the finished square. For example, if you want a square of net 10 meshes wide and 10 meshes deep, continue increasing until you have 11 loops.

Work one row without increasing.

Decreasing rows:	the next row starts the decreasing rows. Net until you get to the last two loops of the previous row and then pick these 2 loops up together in the one knot. In subsequent rows gradually decrease by knotting the last 2 loops of each row together. On the final row knot the 2 remaining loops together and remove the mesh stick before pulling the knot tight.

Cut off the knot forming the foundation loop and join the first 2 stitches together by knotting the foundation thread tightly around the first 2 loops.

The net will need to be blocked. To do this, dampen it and pin it out so that it is square, and leave it to dry.

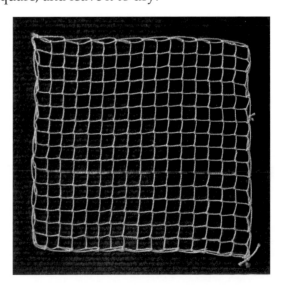

Sample of square netting.

Rectangular piece of netting

Proceed as for a square, increasing at the end of each row until the loops number one more than the number required for the width of the rectangle. Work one plain row, without increasing or decreasing. Increase at the end of the next row, and decrease at the end of the following row. Continue in this way, alternately increasing and decreasing, until the longer side is the desired length.* Then decrease in every row until two loops remain. Join these together as above.

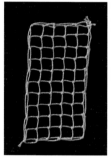

Rectangular
netting sample.

* *Note.* If you want to net an exact number of meshes for the width and the length, you may need to insert a plain row here. To explain further – if the length and width of the rectangle are both an even number of meshes (for example, 10 x 6 meshes), or both an uneven number of meshes (for example 11 x 5 meshes), no plain row is needed. If the length and width are one an even number and the other uneven (for example 10 x 5 meshes), then you will need to insert the plain row.

Guide to making fine square netting

To make fine netting it is necessary to use a double-pointed knitting needle rather than a mesh stick. Here is a guide to the size of knitting needle required to get a square mesh of a particular size (6 holes per inch or smaller). The guide is approximate only, as the size of the thread also has a slight effect.

3 mm needle = 6 holes per inch net
2.5 mm needle = 7 holes per inch net
2 mm needle = 8 holes per inch net
1.75 mm needle = 10 holes per inch net
1.5 mm needle = 12 holes per inch net
1.25 mm needle = 14 holes per inch net
1 mm needle = 16 holes per inch net

Circular netting

Begin with a foundation loop. Leaving a tail longer than the anticipated radius of the completed circle, knot a number of loops into the foundation loop. The number of loops will depend on the pattern, but should be one less than the required number of loops for the first round (see diagram 8a, where the number of loops in the first round will be 12). The joining loop (see below), which brings the working thread to the beginning of the next round will form the last loop, thus making the correct number of loops in the first round. The knots should slide along the foundation loop, but should not be too loose.

Remove the mesh stick. Remove the foundation loop from the pins, and cut off the knot which forms it into a loop. Tie a reef knot in the foundation thread right up close to the netting knots, thus pulling the knots into a tight circle. Re-tie the ends to reform the foundation loop.

Make the joining loop by knotting the working thread and the tail together (diagram 8b) by means of a double overhand knot or a drop knot. The joining loop must be as close as possible to the same size as the other loops. The same method is used at the end of each round to get to the beginning of the next round (diagram 8c). This is the reason for leaving a long tail when you begin, as this tail is gradually carried through the work to the outer edge. Once the piece of netting is completed it should be blocked.

Diagram 8

Beginning a
circle of netting.

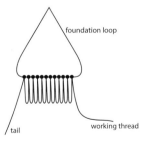

a

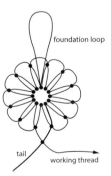

b

c

Practice circle

Round 1: .... make 11 loops into the foundation loop, plus a joining loop (thus making a total of 12 loops).

Round 2: .... make 2 knots in the first loop (this constitutes an increase), and then 1 knot in the next loop. Continue in this fashion, working alternately 2 knots and 1 knot, to the end of the round.

Subsequent rounds: .... make 2 knots into each increase of the preceding round, and 1 knot in every other loop.

Note: The loop that I have referred to here as the 'increase of the preceding round', I sometimes call a 'closed loop', as it does not spread as the normal loops do, but is closed tight top and bottom and forms a narrow loop.

Practice circle

Forming the joining loop

As described above, the joining loop (sometimes known as the connecting loop) joins the working thread to the tail, and brings the working thread to a position ready to start the next round. Any firm knot can be used (such as an overhand knot, but definitely not a granny knot). A good knot to use, because it helps to get the joining loop the correct size, is the drop knot.

The drop knot

Remove all the loops except the last from the mesh stick. With the tail behind the mesh stick and the working thread in front, slide the right-hand end of the mesh stick through the first loop of the previous round (this helps to position the drop knot at the correct place). Loop the working thread around the tail (i.e. a half hitch – diagram 9a), and then tug on the working thread so that the half hitch reforms itself on the working thread (diagram 9b). Slide the knot up to the bottom of the mesh stick and hold it in position with the thumb and forefinger of the left hand.

Remove the mesh stick and complete the drop knot as follows. Take the working thread to the left, then loop it across the front of both threads, around behind them, and finally bring it out to the front again (diagram 9c). Gradually pull the knot tight. You are now ready to start the next round.

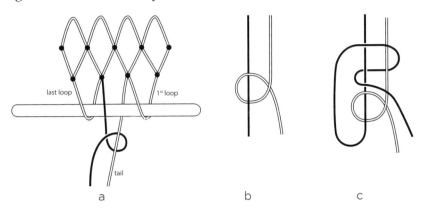

Diagram 9 The drop knot. The working thread is shaded dark.

Joining in new threads

New threads can be joined in by knotting the new thread to the old thread with a lace knot. Alternatively, you can join in a new thread by making a knot with the new thread alongside the last knot of the old thread.

The lace knot: make a slip knot near the start of the new thread. Slide the end of the old thread through the loop of the slip knot. Tighten the slip knot, positioning it where you want the join to be, and then give the two ends of the new thread (a and b in diagram 10) a sharp pull, thus making it grip around the old thread. You should hear a slight click. If the knot has gripped correctly, the new thread will not slide along the old thread.

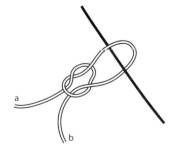

Diagram 10 The lace knot.

CHAPTER 3
Stitches

There are many stitches that can be used in netting. In this book I describe various stitches, but by searching through old books on netting you could find·others that are not listed here. Sometimes, of course, the same stitch can go by different names in different books. Just some of the many different stitches are shown here.

For most of the following samples I used a mesh stick to form the loops, but a double-pointed kitting needle could be used if you want a smaller pattern.

Double and triple stitches

A double stitch is made by wrapping the thread once around the mesh stick and then netting into the next loop. A triple stitch is made by wrapping the thread twice around the mesh stick and then netting into the next loop. Double and triple stitches are a means of making longer loops in among the smaller single loops. Of course, the loop can be made even longer by doing more wraps around the mesh stick.

Making double and triple stitches.

Crossed stitches

There are two main ways of working crossed stitches.

Crossed stitch method 1

The loops are worked in reverse order. When working along a row of netting, net into the 2nd loop first, and then net into the 1st loop. The 2nd loop can either be taken through the first loop before netting, or behind the 1st loop (see diagram 11). Continue along the row in this fashion.

Types of netting which use this method include cross netting, spider netting, honeycomb netting and herringbone netting.

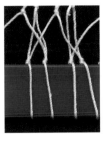

Diagram 11 Crossed stitches, method 1.

Crossed stitch method 2

The loops are worked in the correct order (i.e. 1st, then 2nd) but are intertwined before being netted into.

When working along a row of netting, take the 1st loop through the 2nd and net into it. Take the 2nd loop through the 1st and net into it (see diagram 12). Continue along the row in this fashion.

Rose or Grecian netting is an example of this type of netting.

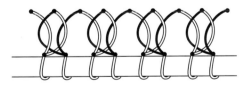
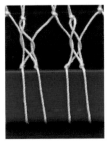

Diagram 12 Crossed stitches, method 2. The first loop of each pair is shown in white, the second loop in black.

Cross netting/stripe netting/herringbone netting

This is the basic pattern which uses the first method of working crossed stitches, and the next two stitches listed below are variations on this. The appearance of the various stitches can vary depending on whether you use a large or small mesh stick or a combination of both.

Cast on an even number of loops.

Row 1:..................plain.

Row 2:..................net into the 2nd loop, then the 1st, then the 4th, then the 3rd, etc. to end of row. Keep repeating rows 1 and 2.

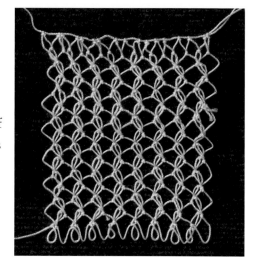

Herringbone netting

Honeycomb netting

Cast on an even number of loops.

Row 1:..................plain.

Row 2:..................net into the 2nd loop, then the 1st, then the 4th, then the 3rd, etc. to end of row.

Row 3:..................plain.

Row 4:..................net 1 plain, and then work as row 2, and end with one plain stitch.

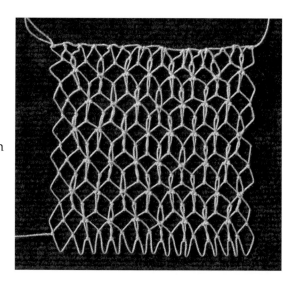

Honeycomb netting

Spider netting

This is really the same as the basic stitch, except that it is bordered by rows of smaller mesh plain netting. An even number of stitches is required. Use two mesh sticks, one large, one small.

With the small mesh stick work a number of rows plain.

Change to large mesh stick.

1st row:..............plain.

2nd row:..............net into the 2nd loop, then the 1st, then the 4th, then the 3rd, etc. to end of row. (small mesh stick) work a number of rows plain.

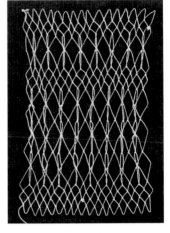

Spider netting

Rose or Grecian netting

This uses the second method of working crossed stitches. Cast on an even number of stitches. The loops of the first row should be larger than those of the second row, so use a mesh stick and a knitting needle, or else make double stitches for the row with the large loops. For the samples illustrated I used a 2 mm knitting needle and a 6 mm mesh stick.

1st row:..............(mesh stick) plain.

2nd row:..............(needle) draw the 1st loop up through the 2nd and net into it. Draw the 2nd loop up through the 1st and net into it. Repeat to end of row.

3rd row:..............(mesh stick) plain.

4th row:..............(needle) net 1, *draw the 1st loop up through the 2nd and net into it. Draw the 2nd loop up through the 1st and net into it*, net 1.

Repeat rows 1 to 4 as many times as desired.

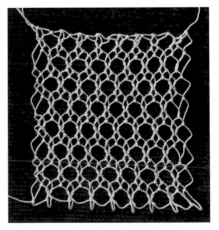

Rose netting

Alternative version of rose or Grecian netting

This netting is the same as the one above except that the holes are directly under each other rather than offset.

Work rows 1 and 2 above, and just keep repeating.

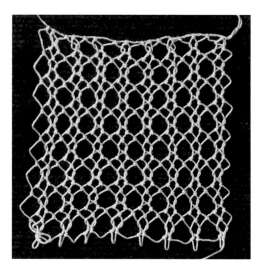

Rose netting

Round netting

Proceed as for normal netting, except that when you draw the netting needle through you do not bring it up through the loop of the previous row. Instead, after bringing the needle through the loop around your hand, you then bring it down through the loop of the previous row – that is, you bring it through the loop of the previous row in the opposite direction from normal, thus getting a twisted loop. The thread coming from the base of the needle should be kept to the right of the needle. Complete the knot as normal.

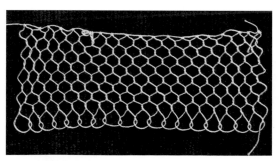

How to work round netting

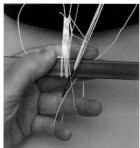

Round netting detail

Puff netting

This is a stitch I found in an old netting book. I used it to make a scarf (see pattern on page 62).

Cast on a multiple of 10 loops. The pattern is made up of 5 rows.

Row 1: ....(an increase row) *net 9, net 9 knots in next loop*, repeat to end.
Rows 2-4: ....plain.
Row 5: ....(a decrease row) *net 9 loops together, net 9*, repeat to end.

Repeat these 5 rows until you reach the desired length. You will notice that the increase stitch ('net 9 knots in next loop') is always done in the loop beneath and immediately to the right of the decrease on the previous row.

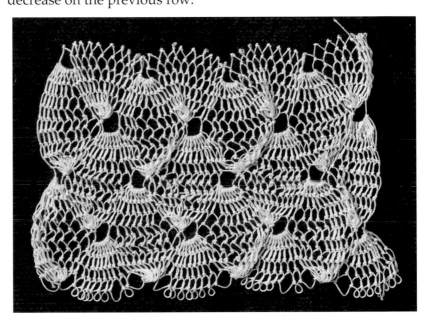

Puff netting

Loop stitch

For loop stitch I used a knitting needle instead of a mesh stick because this stitch looks better with small loops.

Cast on a number of double stitches.

Row 1: ....*wrap thread once around knitting needle and net into the next loop, net another knot into the same loop (i.e. make a small loop)*, repeat to end of row.

| Row 2: | *wrap thread once around knitting needle and net into the next large loop, net another knot into the same loop, miss the small loop*, repeat to end of row. |

Repeat row 2 as many times as desired.

Variation

| Row 1: | *wrap thread once around the knitting needle and net into the next loop, net another 2 knots into the same loop*, repeat to end of row. This gives 2 small loops in between each longer loop. |
| Row 2: | *wrap thread once around the knitting needle and net into the next large loop, net another 2 knots into the same loop, miss the small loops*, repeat to end of row. |

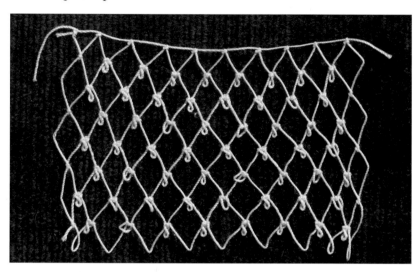

Loop stitch.

Clusters

These are made by joining loops together. There are a number of different ways to do this, and the different ways of joining loops together give different decorative effects.

Clusters method 1

This method joins single loops together to form a point. For an example of this, see the oval mat on page 83. In circular netting a cluster sometimes needs to be made at the beginning of a row and including the knot of the joining loop. In this case you join the required loops together without using the mesh stick. For an example of this see round mat 2, page 69 (row 21).

Clusters made by joining single loops to form a point

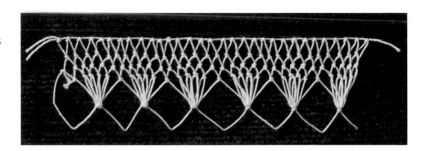

··
In the following examples a cluster of loops is formed by netting a number of times into a single loop. These clusters can then be treated in different ways to get different effects.
··

Clusters method 2

This method joins a cluster of loops together with a preceding or following single loop, which makes the cluster slope to one side. For an example of this, see the rose stitch star mat on page 77.

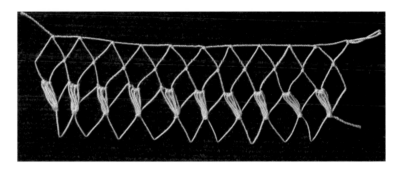

Sloping clusters

Clusters method 3

This method joins half the loops of one group of loops with half the loops of the next group, as well as the intervening loop. The clusters will then slope both to the left and to the right. For an example of this, see round mat 4 on page 71.

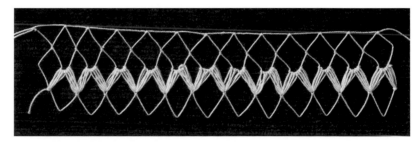

Separated clusters

Clusters method 4

This method joins a cluster of loops without incorporating the preceding or following loop. The clusters can be worked in every loop, or every second loop (as here), or every third loop, etc. Unlike the previous methods, this way of treating the clusters increases the number of overall loops in the row, and can thus be useful for circular mats where you may want to increase the number of loops as the diameter of the mat increases. For an example of this, see miniature doily 3 on page 108.

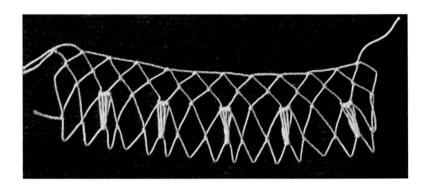

Joining clusters without incorporating preceding or following loop

CHAPTER 4

Edgings

Edgings can be straight, as, for example, a netted strip at opposite ends of a runner or rectangular mat. Or an edging can be the final few rows of a circular mat. Samples of both are given below.

Straight edging of plain square netting

This edging can be used as a base for filet lace embroidery.

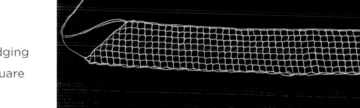

Straight edging of plain square netting

On a foundation loop cast on one more loop than required depth of edging (e.g. the edging illustrated is 7 meshes high, so 8 loops were cast on at the beginning).

Row 1: .... increase 1 stitch at the end of the row.

Row 2: .... decrease 1 stitch at the end of the row.

Repeat until the edging is the required length.

This method gives you sloping edges at either end (as shown in the photograph). The edges can be trimmed to make them straight. However, if you wish to avoid this, you can work the edging as you would for netting a rectangle.

Alternative method of working straight edging

Work as for netting a rectangle.

Begin with 2 stitches on a foundation loop. Increase at the end of each row until you have one more loop than the required depth of the edging. Then repeat rows 1 and 2 above until the edging is the required length. Work one plain row. Then decrease at the end of each row until 2 loops remain. Net these 2 loops together without using the mesh stick.

Sample of a netted edging, embroidered with darning stitch, and sewn to a hand towel. As the thread used for netting was white to match the towel, the netting is not obvious and the blue design stands out. See Appendix 1, page 122, for the filet pattern.

Pointed edgings

Square netting

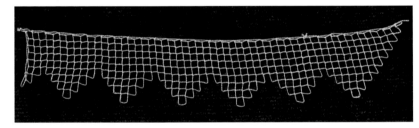

Pointed edging of square netting

This edging is also made from plain square netting. Start as for making a square of net. After the initial few rows and once shaping is started, the rows alternate between a row where there is an increase at the end of the row (at the top edge of the border) and a row where there is no increase (at the stepped side of the border). These plain rows and increasing rows are continued until the depth of the border is the required size, at which stage the next non-increase row becomes a short row, stopping a number of loops before the end of the row.

For a border 9 meshes deep at its widest point, cast on 2 loops and work normal square netting until there are 10 loops, then proceed as follows:

Row 1: ....net 6, turn.
Row 2: ....net to end, netting twice into last loop.
Row 3: ....net 7, turn.
Row 4: ....net to end, netting twice into last loop.
Row 5: ....net 8, turn.
Row 6: ....net to end, netting twice into last loop.
Row 7: ....net 9, turn.
Row 8: ....net to end, netting twice into last loop.

Repeat rows 1–8 until the border is the required length.

Diamond netting

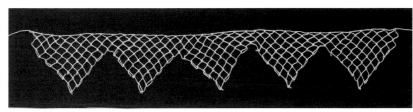

Pointed edging of diamond netting

Cast on a number of loops onto the foundation loop. Work a row or two. To form the points you work into the first loop without the mesh stick (i.e. decrease 1) and then continue with normal netting.

For an edging with five points, cast on 35 loops.
Work 3 plain rows.
Then begin the points as follows:

Row 4: ....decrease 1, net 6.
Row 5: ....decrease 1, net 5.
Row 6: ....decrease 1, net 4.
Row 7: ....decrease 1, net 3.
Row 8: ....decrease 1, net 2.
Row 9: ....decrease 1, net 1.
Row 10: ....decrease 1 (this row could be omitted).

This forms the first point. Cut thread and join it to the next loop of row 3, net 6, then continue from row 5 above.
Work the other points in the same way. For an example of this edging see the Swiss diamond mat on page 82.

Diamond netting variation

Variation of
diamond netting
edging

Instead of decreasing at the beginning of each point, you can decrease by omitting to net into the last loop of each point. This gives a pointed edging with free-floating loops along the edges (like picots), instead of straight edges.

Work as for the first method for the first 3 rows, then:

Row 4: ....net 6, turn.

Row 5: ....net 5, turn.

Row 6: ....net 4, turn.

Row 7: ....net 3, turn.

Row 8: ....net 2, turn.

Row 9: ....net 1.

This forms the first point. Cut thread and join it to the next loop of row 3. Work rows 4–9 again.

Work the other points in the same way.

For an example of this edging see the Shades of Blue mat on page 85.

Scalloped edgings

Scalloped edgings are often referred to as fan or shell edgings.

Scalloped edging 1

Equipment: 2 mm knitting needle; 4 mm mesh stick

Cast on a multiple of 4 loops plus 1.

Row 1: ....(needle) plain.

Row 2: ....(needle) plain.

Row 3: ....(mesh stick) 3 knots in each loop.

Row 4: ....(needle) net 3 together.

Row 5: ....(needle) plain.

Row 6: ....(mesh stick) *8 knots in one loop, wind thread once around mesh stick, miss 3 loops*, repeat, end with 8 knots in last loop.

Row 7: ....(needle) *1 knot in each loop of the cluster (i.e. net 7), take long loop through centre loop of 3 missed loops of previous row and net into it*, repeat, net 8 at end of row.

Row 8: ....(needle) plain.

Row 9: ....(needle) net 6, *net 3 together, net 5*, repeat to end, except net 7 in final scallop (the net 3 together is worked between the scallops).

Scalloped
edging 1

Scalloped edgings 2 and 3

Scalloped edgings 2 and 3 are simple edgings for circular mats. In these examples I have begun with the first 14 rows of round mat 3 on page 70, using a 2.5 mm knitting needle, 6 mm mesh stick, and DMC Cebelia 40.

Row 1: ....(2.5 mm needle) leaving a long tail of thread, make 16 loops into the foundation loop (including the joining loop).

Row 2: ....(2.5 mm needle) plain.

Row 3:	(6 mm mesh stick) 2 knots in joining loop and then 3 knots in each loop.
Rows 4 & 5:	(2.5 mm needle) plain.
Row 6:	(6 mm mesh stick) plain.
Row 7:	(2.5 mm needle) take the joining loop backwards through the last loop and make the first knot into this last loop, *take second loop through the first and knot into this loop, make next knot into the first loop (i.e. crossed loops)*, repeat to end of row.
Row 8:	(2.5 mm needle) 1 knot in joining loop and then 2 knots in each loop.
Rows 9 & 10:	(2.5 mm needle) plain.
Row 11:	(6 mm mesh stick) plain.
Row 12:	(2.5 mm needle) as row 7.
Rows 13 & 14:	(2.5 mm needle) plain.

Scalloped edging 2

Row 15:	(6 mm mesh stick) *miss one loop, 6 knots into next loop, miss one loop, 1 knot into next loop*, repeat.
Rows 16 & 17:	(2.5 mm needle) plain.
Row 18:	(2.5 mm needle) *knot 2 loops together, net 5,* repeat.

Scalloped edging 2

Scalloped edging 3

Row 15: ....(6 mm mesh stick) 3 knots in joining loop, *miss 3 loops, 4 knots into next loop,* repeat.

Row 16: ....(2.5 mm needle) take joining loop back through the middle loop of the 3 missed loops, *net into each of the next 3 long loops, take the next long loop through the middle loop of the 3 missed loops and net into it*, repeat.

Scalloped edging 3

Pineapple edging

Pineapple edging was a very popular edging that was used in many old designs. It is used for round mat 3 on page 70.

Pineapple edging

Other simple edgings for circular mats

Circular edging 1

Alternate 1 plain stitch and 1 double stitch (i.e. wrap the thread once around the mesh stick before netting into the next loop). It is used for round mat 1 (the beginner's piece) on page 68.

Simple circular edging 1

Circular edging 2

This edging uses clusters. When you have a lot of loops close together towards the outer edge of a doily, you can simply gather the loops into clusters to form the last row. This method is used in miniature doilies 1 and 4 (see pages 106 and 109).

Two examples of simple circular edging 2

Circular edging 3

Another use of clusters. In the second to last row work a number of loops in each loop of the preceding row (e.g. 6 loops). In the final row gather the loops into clusters by taking half the loops from one group and half from the next group (i.e. take the last 3 loops from one 6-loop group and the first 3 loops from the next 6-loop group). This is used in miniature doily 2 on page 107.

Circular edging 4

In the second to last row work plain netting. In the last row use a larger mesh stick and work into every alternate loop. This is used in miniature doily 6 on page 110.

Simple circular edging 3

Simple circular edging 4

Circular edging 5

In the second to last row use a large mesh stick or knitting needle, and make long loops. In the last row use a smaller mesh stick or knitting needle, and make short loops. This is used in miniature doily 5 on page 110.

Simple circular edging 5

CHAPTER 5
Advanced techniques

Swiss diamond netting

I have placed Swiss diamond netting among the advanced techniques because it requires you to adapt the usual technique for making the netting knot. This may be a little difficult to master at first, but it is well worth the effort, as it then allows you to work interesting patterns. The Swiss diamond mat, page 82, and the Rings of Fire bag, page 97, make use of this technique.

In Swiss diamond netting you have some loops which are longer than the rest in the row. When you net into these loops your knot is not always formed in the middle of the loop and does not always sit nicely on top of the mesh stick. The two important stitches for this technique I have given the names 'left long loop' and 'right long loop'.

The **left long loop** is quite simple to work. Remove your mesh stick from the previous stitches and knot into the long loop of the previous row in the usual way. At the beginning of a sequence of Swiss diamond netting this means that you will net into the centre of the long loop (as in row 2 of the practice piece below), but in following rows (rows 3–5) the knot will be to the right of centre.

The **right long loop** is a little more difficult. Keeping the mesh stick in the loop you have just made, you make a knot in the usual way into the next small loop of the previous row, but when it comes to tightening the knot, you do not pull the thread down towards yourself. Instead of positioning the knot at the top of the mesh stick, pull the thread up, away from yourself, until it is sitting in the centre of the small loop at a distance above the mesh stick. You need to hold the knot in position with the index finger and thumb of your left hand while you continue to pull the thread up away from yourself until the knot is tight.

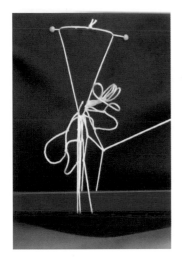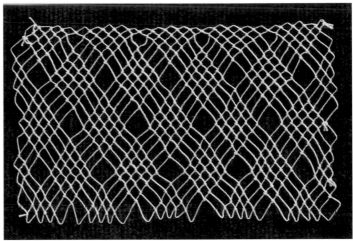

Left: Position of knot for right long stitch Right: Swiss diamond practice piece

Practice piece

Cast on a multiple of 5 loops, plus 4 (pictured sample has 24 loops).

Row 1: net 4, *1 double stitch, net 4*.

Row 2: 1 double stitch, net 3, *1 left long stitch, 1 right long stitch, net 3*.

Row 3: 1 double stitch, net 2, *1 left long stitch, net 1, 1 right long stitch, net 2*, end with 1 left long loop.

Row 4: net 1, 1 right long stitch, net 1, 1 left long stitch, *net 2, 1 right long stitch, net 1, 1 left long stitch*.

Row 5: net 1, 1 right long stitch, 1 left long stitch, *net 3, 1 right long stitch, 1 left long stitch*, end with net 1.

Row 6: net 2, *1 double stitch, net 4*, end with 1 double stitch, net 1.

Row 7: net 1, *1 left long stitch, 1 right long stitch, net 3*, end with 1 left long stitch, 1 right long stitch, net 1.

Row 8: net 1, *1 left long stitch, net 1, 1 right long stitch, net 2*, omit net 2 on last repeat.

Row 9: net 3, 1 right long stitch, net 1, 1 left long stitch, *net 2, 1 right long stitch, net 1, 1 left long stitch*, end with net 2, 1 right long stitch.

Row 10: 1 left long stitch, *net 3, 1 right long stitch, 1 left long stitch*, end with net 3.

These rows constitute one pattern.

Repeat from row 1.

Note: The basic sequence in rows 1–5 and 6–10 is the same, except that the rows are offset so that the diamonds are not directly under each other.

Swiss diamond motif

Swiss diamond motif

Equipment:	2 mm and 2.5 mm knitting needles, 6 mm and 12 mm mesh sticks
Thread:	Cebelia 40 (Cebelia 30 could be used for a heavier mat)

Row 1: (2 mm needle) cast on 15 loops.

Row 2: (6 mm mesh stick) plain.

Row 3: (2 mm needle) net 2 in each loop.

Rows 4 & 5: (2 mm needle) plain.

Row 6: (2 mm needle) net 1, *1 double stitch, net 4*, repeat to end of row ending with 1 double stitch, net 3 (i.e. in this row you will have 4 small loops followed by one large loop).

Rows 7-10: (2 mm needle) Swiss diamond netting.

Row 11: (12 mm mesh stick) net 2 in each loop.

Row 12: (2.5 mm needle) plain.

Square diamond netting

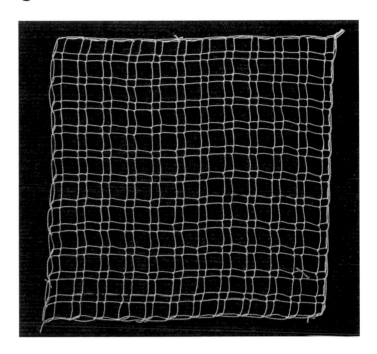

Square diamond netting

As with normal square netting, you increase at the end of each row for the first half of the square, work the middle row without increasing, and then decrease in the following rows by netting the last 2 stitches together. Finish off by netting the last 2 stitches together without the mesh stick.

Row 1: .... cast on 1 plain stitch, 1 double stitch.

Row 2: .... net 1 plain stitch, in next loop make 2 right long stitches (i.e. stitch is made away from the needle).

Row 3: .... 1 plain, 1 double stitch, 1 plain, 1 double stitch.

Row 4: .... *1 plain, 1 right long stitch*, repeat, end with another right long stitch.

Row 5: .... *1 plain, 1 double stitch*, repeat to end of row.

Row 6: .... *1 plain, 1 right long stitch*, repeat to end of row, ending with another right long stitch.

Repeat rows 5 and 6 until you reach the desired size, ending with row 5.

Centre row: .... (an even row) *1 plain, 1 right long stitch*, repeat to end of row (do not increase).

Now start the decreasing rows, joining the last 2 loops together in each row.

1st decreasing row:....................1 plain, *1 plain, 1 double stitch*.

2nd decreasing row:....................*1 plain, 1 right long stitch*.

Repeat these two rows until you get down to 2 loops. Join these loops together.

Finnish konu stitch

This is a stitch that I learnt at a filet lace workshop in Finland. I have used this stitch in the Konu mat on page 94. The stitch allows you to form a pattern of larger holes in otherwise regular filet net.

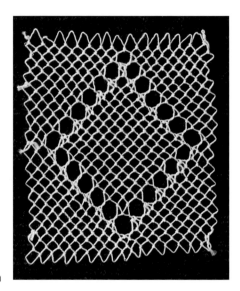

Sample of Finnish konu stitch

1st row:.................net as normal, but where the hole is to be, wrap the thread around the mesh stick/knitting needle to make a large loop.

2nd row:.................net as normal. When you get to the large loop, net into the bottom of the large loop (see diagram 13).

Diagram 13

3rd row:.................net as normal. When you get to the large loop, twist the loop from the 2nd row through the large loop of the 1st row and net into it. Do this on both sides of the hole (see diagram 14).

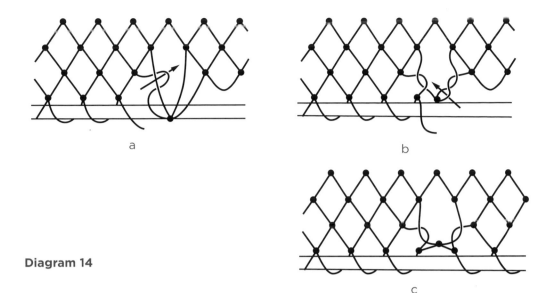

Diagram 14

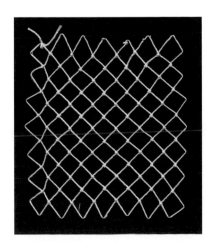

When you are doing a diamond or zigzag pattern of konu holes (i.e. where the holes are in consecutive rows), for the second row of holes do the wrap for the new holes on the 3rd row of the first konu (i.e. you do a wrap immediately before and after doing the twisted stitches).

Working a square of diamond netting

If you work a plain length of diamond netting you will notice that the loops on either side of the piece of netting do not line up (they alternate). It is impossible to get an exact square. To get a square you can use the following methods.

Square of diamond netting, method 1

Method 1: square of diamond netting, 7 loops along each side

This method gives you a single square at each of the corners. The centre of this square also is a single mesh of the net, and so this method is useful for darning filet patterns which have an uneven number of meshes in the design.

Knot your thread to the foundation loop, leaving a tail so that you can knot it to your finishing thread. Cast on one less loop than the required finished number (i.e. if you want 7 loops along each side start with 6 loops. Work rows of plain netting until you have the required number of loops down the *right* hand side (the number of rows, including the cast-on row, will be double the required number of loops – in this sample 14 rows). You should finish on the same side of the net as the initial knot. Now remove the foundation loop and make a new foundation loop by weaving a thread through the loops on the side of the net (the opposite side to where you have finished). Now work up the side (left side on picture above), finishing by knotting your beginning and ending threads together to form the final loop. You will now have an equal number of loops on each side.

Square of diamond netting, method 2

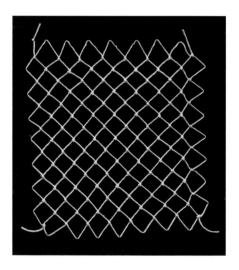

Method 2: square of diamond netting, 7 loops along each side

This method gives you corners which consist of two squares on an angle. The centre of this square comes at an intersection and so the centre is a block of 4 meshes, thus this method is useful for darning filet patterns which have an even number of meshes in the design.

Knot your thread to the foundation loop and cast on the exact number of loops of the required finished number (i.e. 7 loops). Work rows of plain netting until you have the required number of loops down the left side (do not count what appears to be a small loop coming from the initial knot, because once the foundation thread is taken away, this apparent loop disappears). The number of rows will be double the required number of loops plus 2 (in this sample 16 rows). Once again you should finish on the same side of the net as the initial knot. Cut the thread.

Remove foundation loop and make a new foundation loop up the side (this time on the same side as your beginning and ending knots). Knot your thread to the bottom loop (on the other side from where you have just finished) and work up the side (right side on picture above), finishing by knotting into the last loop of your first row.

This technique can also be used to get a regular rectangle (as in the miniature mat on page 112) or an octagon (as in the octagonal mat on page 113).

Octagons

You can get an octagon shape quite simply in this way:

Cast on a certain number of loops on a foundation thread. Work a number of rows, increasing at the end of each row until the netting is the width you want, and then work a number of plain rows without increasing. When this is at the desired length, work a number of rows decreasing at the end of each row until you are down to the same number of loops you started with. However, you will find that this octagon is not completely symmetrical. This may not matter if you are working a large piece, but if you are making a small piece where exactness is important, it could be a problem.

If you want a symmetrical octagon you can use the method used for working a square of diamond netting. Work the first part of the octagon as described above – that is, cast on loops on the foundation thread, and work increasing rows, followed by plain rows. Once you have finished the plain rows (making sure that you finish the plain rows on the side with the lesser number of loops), work up the side of the net until you get to the loop where you started the plain rows. Cut the thread. You will now have the same number of loops on each side.

Put the foundation thread back on its pins, join in the thread at the bottom of the work and work one plain row. For the succeeding rows decrease at the beginning of each row (i.e. make the 1st knot without using a mesh stick), until you have the required number of loops left. Join the last 2 loops of the first row together (this can be done when working the border, if a border is to be worked) – this gives the required number of loops along the top.

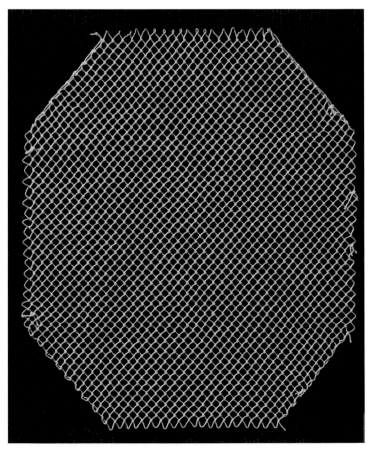

Octagon

Ovals

To make an oval piece of net, you need to make an oval centre, and then you can just work around the oval as you would around a circle. There are a number of different ways to achieve an oval centre, and four are described here.

Oval method 1

The simplest method is to increase at opposite sides of the beginning circle.

Simple oval, method 1

Oval method 2

Start as for a circular centre. When the desired size is reached, remove the foundation thread and loosen the knots. The loops are then divided into four groups. Using a needle (e.g. a tapestry needle) and thread, one group is knotted together, forming a cluster at one end of the oval. Then the loops of the two groups on either side of this first group are joined to each other one by one, forming the straight centre of the mat (see diagram 15).

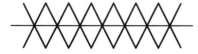

Diagram 15 Joining loops to make the centre.
Oval method 2

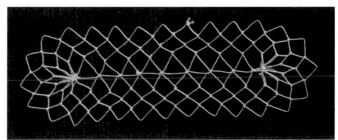

Finally, the group at the other end of the oval is joined together with a knot, forming a second cluster. This technique was used for the miniature oval doily on page 112.

Oval method 3

Work a length of diamond netting. Then shape one end by decreasing in the centre:

work one row with a decrease at the centre by netting 2 loops together, two rows plain, repeat once more. Then decrease in the centre of every row until there are 3 loops left. Knot these loops together. Cut the foundation loop and slide it out. The knots where the netting joined the foundation loop can now be popped out by pushing on them with a knitting needle, leaving a row of plain loops.

Put in a new foundation thread above these loops. Join in a new thread and work the same number of plain rows as you did for the other side. Then shape this end in the same way as the other side.

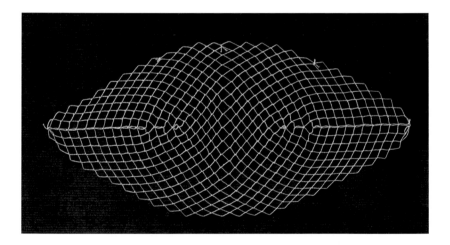

Oval method 3

Oval method 4

Start with a circle in the centre and then work on one side of the circle, extending it into an oval shape, and repeating this on the other side of the circle. There are a number of variations on this technique.

Two examples of oval centres. The one on the left was used for the oval mat (see page 83). For the one on the right you start with a circle, increasing at four evenly spaced places. Once you have done a few rows, you then work on one side only; when you have finished that side, you work on the other side to make the oval.

After working the oval centre you join your thread to one of the loops and then go on to work the outer section of the mat. It is more difficult to work an oval mat than a circular mat from the initial foundation loop. I find it easier to work the first few rows of the outer section by pinning the oval centre to the pillow rather than using the foundation loop. As you work around the oval you can shift the pins into the most convenient position. After you have worked a few rows you can then thread a new foundation loop through the loops where the outer section joins the original oval centre. As you work around the oval during the outer rows, this new foundation loop can be slipped around to the most convenient position for working.

Linking loops together instead of knotting

Linking loops together instead of knotting in itself is not difficult, but I have included it here because it is rather unusual. It is a useful technique which I have employed for some items in the pattern section.

Grecian stitch with plain netting border

I have used two different coloured threads for this sample, so that it is easier to see how linking loops is done. I used a knitting needle to make this sample, but a mesh stick could be used.

Grecian stitch with plain netting border

With the pink thread cast on 18 loops (4 loops on either side for plain netting, 10 loops for Grecian/rose stitch).

Rows 1–3: plain.

Row 4: net 14, turn. Now work only on the centre 10 stitches.

Row 5: *wrap thread around the knitting needle, net 1*, 10 times.

Row 6: *take 1st loop through 2nd and net into it, take 2nd loop though 1st and net into it*, 5 times.

Repeat rows 5 and 6 four more times. Cut thread (leaving a tail).

Side borders

Note that one side has one less row worked than on the other side.

1st side: on the side with fewer rows join the thread in by working a knot in the edge of the Grecian stitch section, net 4.

Work 15 plain rows (4 stitches to each row). On every row

that ends at the inside edge (i.e. next to the Grecian stitch centre section) link the two sections by threading the thread through the Grecian stitch section before working the next row. Knot the thread with the tail of the Grecian stitch section.

2nd side: knot the thread into the Grecian stitch section and work down this side with plain netting, linking the two sections together as you did on the other side. Work a total of 15 rows. Turn and then work plain netting across the entire width [18 loops]. Work 3 more rows. Cut thread.

This technique works best if you work a sufficient number of rows in the Grecian stitch section to result in an odd number of rows with large holes.

Other advanced techniques

Some of the patterns in the pattern section use techniques which can be described as advanced. For example, the scarf pattern on page 63 has a border of small loops but incorporates long loops into the centre of the scarf. See the pattern for instructions on how to do this.

Another advanced technique is tassel stitch, used in the tassel stitch doily on page 101.

Changing colours in a piece can be as simple as changing the colour at the beginning of a new row, but it can be more complicated than this, as is shown by this sample, where squares of different colours are joined together in an alternating pattern. This technique is explained in the chequerboard mat on page 92. The pattern combines two techniques explained above, that is, making exact squares of diamond netting, and linking loops together.

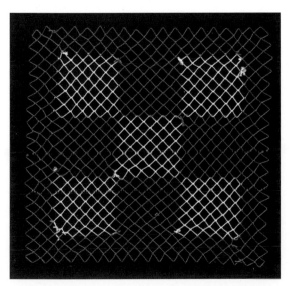

Example of a chequerboard design

Section 2
Patterns

*For this section I have designed a number of patterns, ranging from bulky scarves,
made with thick threads, down to tiny miniature doilies made with very fine threads.
Hopefully you will find something here to suit your fancy.*

CHAPTER 6
Scarves and shawls

The scarves included in this chapter are just samples of what you can do with netting. You can design your own scarves, choosing stitches from the first part of this book. You could also make vests or jackets. I have listed the threads I used for the scarves, but availability varies, and you can substitute threads of your choice. As the scarves are made with wool and other bulky threads, it is necessary to use one of the larger plastic shuttles rather than a steel netting needle.

Scarves can be started in the normal way with a foundation loop pinned to a pillow, but as the scarf gets longer you can wrap it around the pillow to keep it firm for working on. Once the desired length is reached, cut the foundation loop and slide it out. The knots which are left at the top of the scarf are now no longer attached to anything, and can easily be loosened by inserting a knitting needle into the loop and pulling on the loop. The knots 'pop out' and plain loops are left. A fringe can be attached to these loops and to the loops at the bottom of the scarf.

Herringbone netting scarf

Equipment: 24 mm mesh stick

Thread: Patons Zhivago, 2 balls

Cast on 26 loops. Work one row plain. Work the following rows in herringbone stitch, but begin and end each row with a plain stitch (i.e. net 1, herringbone stitch for 24 loops, net 1). When the scarf is the desired length work a final plain row. Add a fringe to the top and bottom.

Round netting scarf

Equipment: 24 mm mesh stick

Thread: Patons Wilderness, 2 balls

Cast on 18 loops. Work 65 rows (or desired length) in round netting. Remove the foundation thread and pop out the knots.

Twist the scarf once, and then join the ends together to make a circle as follows. Pin the middle of the

scarf to the pillow, and work another row. Before working each stitch take the netting needle through the corresponding loop of the first row, and then work the knot in the usual way. Continue like this to the end of the row. The first and last rows will thus be linked together to form a circle, although they will not be knotted together.

To make a normal scarf, just work rows until the scarf is the required length and then add a fringe each end.

Puff netting scarf

Equipment:	20 mm and 10 mm mesh sticks
Thread:	4-ply wool, 1–2 balls depending on length of scarf

Cast on 30 loops with the 20 mm mesh stick. Work one row plain. These two rows (the cast-on row and the plain row) form a foundation which will be removed once the scarf is the required length (they could be worked in a different colour so that it is easier to see which threads are to be cut when removing the foundation rows).

Join in the wool and start the puff netting.

Row 1:	(an increase row) *net 9, net 9 knots in next loop*, repeat to end.
Rows 2–4:	plain.
Row 5:	(a decrease row) *net 9 loops together, net 9*, repeat to end.

Repeat these five rows until the scarf is the length you wish. Finish with a decrease row and then work a plain row, except that you work 2 loops together beneath the clusters of the previous row.

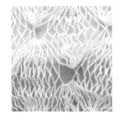

Change to the 10 mm mesh stick and work another plain row, again working 2 loops together immediately beneath the decrease stitch of the previous row.

Go to the beginning of the scarf and remove the foundation rows. With the scarf now turned upside down (so that the top has become the bottom), join in the thread and with the 20 mm mesh stick work a plain row, but joining two threads together beneath the clusters (the increase stitches) of the first row, as you did at the other end of the scarf. Change to the 10 mm mesh stick and work another plain row, again working two loops together immediately beneath the decrease stitch of the previous row. If you want a more solid, less airy look, you could use a thicker wool, or you could use a smaller mesh stick.

Scarf with long loop centre and short loop border

Equipment: 10 mm mesh stick and 39 mm plastic ruler

Thread: Patons Lite Inca (50% wool, 30% acrylic, 20% alpaca), 2 balls

For this scarf I used a plastic ruler as a mesh stick to get the required width. The larger mesh stick needs to be approximately four times the size of the smaller mesh stick.

Row 1: (small mesh stick) cast on 24 loops.

Row 2: (small mesh stick) plain.

Row 3: (small mesh stick) net 4, turn, net 4, turn, net 4, (change to large mesh stick), net 16 (the centre 16 loops), (change to small mesh stick), net 4, turn, net 4, turn, net 4.

Rows 4 & 5: (small mesh stick) plain across full width.

Repeat rows 3–5 as many times as required to get the desired length.

Complete the scarf by adding a fringe at both ends.

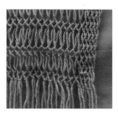

Grecian stitch scarf with plain border

Equipment: 14 mm mesh stick

Thread: Moda Vera Pure Wool extra twist, 2 balls

Row 1:   cast on 29 loops.
Note: I put on 29 loops so that I could have a 4-stitch border on one side and a 5-stitch border on the other side. I did this because one side of the centre section has long loops which form another row of holes when looped in with the edge, whereas the other side has shorter loops. If you have 4 stitches both sides, one border looks narrower than the other.

Rows 2 & 3:   plain.

Row 4:   net 25 (leaving last 4 loops), turn.

Row 5:   *wrap thread around needle, net 1*, 20 times, turn (leaving last 5 loops).
Now continue working the Grecian stitch centre section, working on these 20 stitches.

Row 6:   *take 1st loop through 2nd and net into it, take 2nd loop though 1st and net into it*, 10 times.
Repeat rows 5 and 6 four more times.
Work four plain rows.

Work 5 more blocks of 10 rows of Grecian stitch followed by four plain rows. On the last repeat omit the four plain rows. If you want a longer scarf you can work an extra repeat of the pattern.

Plain netting borders

Work these as described on page 56 for the sample piece, Grecian stitch with plain netting border, except that here one side has 4 stitches, the other side 5 stitches.

Work 4 plain rows across the entire bottom [29 stitches].

At the top end, remove the foundation loop, and pop out the knots. Add a fringe to top and bottom.

Purple and beige shawl

For this shawl I worked with three netting needles/shuttles as follows:
Wind the three netting needles/shuttles with your chosen threads. Work one row with one thread. Join in a new thread at the end of the row. Work a row with that thread. Join in the 3rd thread and work the next row with that thread. Now pick up the first netting needle/shuttle and work the 4th row with that thread. Continue in this way, working each row with a different thread. When you finish each row you will have one netting needle/shuttle at the beginning of the row (on your left) and 2 at the end of the row (on your right). When you turn the work to begin a new row, bring the two needles/shuttles across to the beginning of the row (from the right to the left) and the other single needle/shuttle to the end of the row (from the left to the right).

Threads:	I used the following threads, but you can choose any combination that appeals to you. A knobbly thread, such as the Moda Vera Alpaca Virgin Wool Blend, is a bit difficult to work with, but with practice you get used to it.

- Moda Vera Alpaca Virgin Wool Blend, beige
- Moda Vera 100% wool, dark purple
- Heirloom Mohair Mist, mauve (wrapped once around mesh stick)

Equipment:	25 mm mesh stick; 3 netting needles or shuttles (a shuttle is needed for thicker threads, but a large netting needle could be used for finer threads)

Cast on 20 loops. Work as many rows as you like to get the desired length.

CHAPTER 7

Lace

In this chapter I have included designs for traditional netted lace, using finer threads than those used for the scarves. As the threads are finer, steel netting needles can be used instead of the plastic shuttles. The sizes of these needles vary, and you can use whichever size you prefer, but generally it is best to use the bigger needles with thicker threads, and smaller needles with finer threads. The designs at the beginning of the chapter are easy designs, starting with a beginner's piece, and the patterns towards the end are more involved, some also requiring surface embroidery in linen stitch or darning stitch to finish them. Some of the designs are in traditional white or ecru, and others are made with coloured threads. The choice of colour is a personal thing, and you can alter the colours to suit yourself.

When working the round mats always leave a long tail of thread at the beginning (longer than the radius of the mat), so that it can be carried through the mat as the joining thread for each row.

Round mat 1
(beginner's mat)

Finished size: 23 cm (9 in) diameter

Equipment: 3 mm double-pointed knitting needle and 8 mm mesh stick

Thread: Butterfly thread no. 50, or Cebelia 30, or similar thread

Row 1: (8 mm mesh stick) leaving a long tail of thread, cast on 16 loops into the foundation loop (including the joining loop).

Row 2: (8 mm mesh stick) make another knot into the joining loop, and then work 2 knots into each loop.

Rows 3–6: (3 mm needle) plain.

Row 7: (8 mm mesh stick) plain.

Row 8: (8 mm mesh stick) make another knot into the joining loop, and then work 2 knots into each loop.

Rows 9–13: (3 mm needle) plain.

Row 14: (8 mm mesh stick) plain.

Row 15: (8 mm mesh stick) make another knot into the joining loop, and then work 2 knots into each loop.

Rows 16–21: (3 mm needle) plain.

Row 22: (3 mm needle) work 1 knot into each loop of the preceding row, but alternate one long loop with one plain loop. The long loop is worked by wrapping the thread once around the needle before making a knot in the normal way (i.e. a double stitch). Make your last knot alongside the joining loop knot.

Round mat 2

Finished size: 21 cm (8 ¼ in) diameter

Equipment: 12 mm, 6 mm, 4 mm mesh sticks; 2 mm and 2.75 mm double-pointed knitting needles

Thread: crochet cotton no. 40

Row 1: (12 mm mesh stick) cast on 16 loops (including the joining loop).

Rows 2 & 3: (4 mm mesh stick) plain.

Row 4: (6 mm mesh stick) make 3 knots in the joining loop, and then 4 knots in each successive loop.

Row 5: (2 mm needle) plain.

Row 6: (6 mm mesh stick) plain.

Row 7: (2 mm needle) plain.

Row 8: (6 mm mesh stick) plain.

Row 9: (2.75 mm needle) plain.

Row 10: (6 mm mesh stick) plain.

Row 11: (2.75 mm needle) plain.

Row 12: (6 mm mesh stick) plain.

Row 13: (4 mm mesh stick) plain.

Row 14: (6 mm mesh stick) make 3 knots in the joining loop, and then 4 knots in each successive loop.

Rows 15–19: (2 mm needle) plain.

Row 20: (6 mm mesh stick) plain.

Row 21: (6 mm mesh stick) knot the first 2 loops together without using the mesh stick (no loop is formed and the knot is right next to the joining knot, thus joining 3 loops together), *net 1, knot 3 together*, repeat to end of row, ending with net 1 and a joining knot.

Row 22: (2 mm needle) plain. End by making the last knot next to the joining knot.

Round mat 3

Finished size:	20 cm (8 in) diameter
Equipment:	2.5 mm double-pointed knitting needle; 6 mm mesh stick
Thread:	crochet cotton no. 40

Row 1: (2.5 mm needle) cast on 16 loops into the foundation loop (including the joining loop).

Row 2: (2.5 mm needle) plain.

Row 3: (6 mm mesh stick) 2 knots in joining loop and then 3 knots in each loop.

Rows 4 & 5: (2.5 mm needle) plain.

Row 6: (6 mm mesh stick) plain.

Row 7: (2.5 mm needle) take the joining loop backwards through the last loop and make the first knot into this last loop, *take second loop through the first and knot into this loop, make next knot into the first loop (i.e. crossed loops)*, repeat to end of row.

Row 8: (2.5 mm needle) 1 knot in joining loop and then 2 knots in each loop.

Rows 9 & 10: (2.5 mm needle) plain.

Row 11: (6 mm mesh stick) plain.

Row 12: (2.5 mm needle) as row 7.

Rows 13 & 14: (2.5 mm needle) plain.

Row 15: (6 mm mesh stick) plain.

Row 16: (2.5 mm needle) as row 7.

Rows 17–20: (2.5 mm needle) plain.

Row 21: (6 mm mesh stick) make 3 knots in the joining loop, miss 1 loop, then *make 4 knots in next loop, miss 1 loop*, repeat to end of row.

Rows 22 & 23:	(2.5 mm needle) plain.
Row 24:	(2.5 mm needle) *miss 1 loop, net 3*, repeat to end of row, ending with net 2 and a joining loop.
Row 25:	(2.5 mm needle) *miss 1 loop, net 2*, repeat to end of row, ending with net one and a joining loop. Leave the thread a little loose when you do the 'miss 1 loop', so that loop between the groups of 'net 2' is slightly longer than the loose loop of previous row.
Row 26:	(2.5 mm needle) *miss 1 loop, thread around mesh stick, net 1*, repeat to end. Finish off by netting alongside the knot of the joining loop of previous row.

Round mat 4

Finished size:	24 cm (9 ½ in) diameter
Equipment:	8 mm and 6 mm mesh sticks; 2.5 mm double-pointed knitting needle
Thread:	Special Dentelles (or Cebelia 30) For a slightly larger and thicker mat you could use no. 20 crochet cotton and 10 mm, 6 mm and 3 mm mesh sticks.

Row 1:	(6 mm mesh stick) cast on 12 loops (including the joining loop).
Row 2:	(6 mm mesh stick) work 2 knots in the joining loop and then 3 knots in each loop (36 loops).
Rows 3 & 4:	(2.5 mm needle) plain.
Row 5:	(8 mm mesh stick) *miss 1, net 1*, repeat [18 loops].
Row 6:	(6 mm mesh stick) 2 knots in joining loop, *4 knots in each loop*, repeat to end of row, ending with 1 knot in 1st loop (i.e. joining loop), and a new joining loop [72 loops].

Rows 7 & 8:	(2.5 mm needle) plain.
Row 9:	(2.5 mm needle) net 1, *5 knots in next loop, net 3*, repeat to end of row, ending with net 1 and joining loop.
Row 10:	(2.5 mm needle) net 1, *net 3 together twice, net 2*, repeat to end of row, ending with net 3 together twice and a joining loop.
Row 11:	(2.5 mm needle) plain.
Row 12:	(8 mm mesh stick)*miss 1, net 1*, repeat [36 loops].
Row 13:	(6 mm mesh stick) 3 knots in joining loop and then 4 knots in each loop [144 loops].
Rows 14 & 15:	(2.5 mm needle) plain.
Row 16:	(2.5 mm needle) net 2, *5 knots in next loop, net 3*, repeat to end of row, ending with a joining loop but gather the last 2 loops just made in with the joining loop.
Row 17:	(2.5 mm needle) net 2, *net 3 together twice, net 2*, repeat to end of row, ending with net 3 together and a joining loop.
Row 18:	(2.5 mm needle) net 1, *5 knots in next loop, net 3*, repeat to end of row, ending with net 1 and joining loop.
Row 19:	(2.5 mm needle) net 1, *net 3 together twice, net 2*, repeat to end of row, ending with net 3 together twice and a joining loop.
Row 20:	(2.5 mm needle) plain.
Row 21:	(8 mm mesh stick) net into every third loop.
Row 22:	(6 mm mesh stick) 3 knots in the joining loop and then 4 knots in each loop.
Rows 23 & 24:	(2.5 mm needle) plain.
Row 25:	(2.5 mm needle) *miss one loop, net 3*, repeat to end of row, ending with net 2 and a joining loop.
Row 26:	(2.5 mm needle) *miss 1 loop (leave the thread a little loose here so that the loop is slightly longer than the missed loop of the previous row), net 2*, repeat to end of row, ending with net 1 and a joining loop.
Row 27:	(2.5 mm needle) *thread around mesh stick, miss 1 loop, net 1*, repeat to end. Finish off by netting into the joining loop.

The next three designs are variations on a theme. They begin in the same way but then develop differently.

Round mat 5

Finished size: 25 cm (10 in) diameter

Equipment: 6 mm and 4 mm mesh sticks

Thread: Cebelia 30

Row 1: (6 mm mesh stick) cast on 10 loops (including the joining loop).

Row 2: (4 mm mesh stick) plain. Change to 6 mm mesh stick.

Row 3: 4 knots in joining loop, *5 knots in each loop*, repeat to end of row.

Rows 4 & 5: plain.

Row 6: net 1, *net 5 together, net 5*, repeat, ending with net 3, and then a joining loop.

Row 7: plain.

Row 8: work 9 knots in joining loop, *net 2, 10 knots in next loop*, repeat.

Rows 9 & 10: plain.

Row 11: net together without the mesh stick the last 2 loops of previous row, the joining loop and the next two loops, (cluster made), *net 7, net 5 together*, repeat.

Rows 12–14: plain.

Row 15: net 1, *work 9 knots in next loop, net 3*, repeat, ending with net 2 and a joining loop.

Rows 16–18: plain.

Row 19: taking the last loop of the previous row, the joining loop, and the next 5 loops, make a cluster (without the mesh stick), *net 5, net 7 together*, repeat.

Row 20: ....(4 mm mesh stick) net 1 without the mesh stick, *net 4, net 2 together*, repeat, ending with a knot alongside the first knot.

Round mat 6

Finished size: 24 cm (9 1/2 in) diameter

Equipment: 4 mm mesh stick; 2.5 mm double-pointed knitting needle

Thread: DMC Cordonnet 100

Row 1: ....(4 mm mesh stick) cast on 10 loops (including the joining loop).

Row 2: ....(2.5 mm needle) plain. Change to 4 mm mesh stick.

Row 3: ....4 knots in joining loop, *5 knots in each loop*, repeat to end of row.

Rows 4 & 5: ....plain.

Row 6: ....net 1, *net 5 together, net 5*, repeat, ending with net 3, and then a joining loop.

Row 7: ....plain.

Row 8: ....work 9 knots in joining loop, *net 2, 10 knots in next loop*, repeat.

Rows 9 & 10: ....plain.

Row 11: ....net together without the mesh stick, last 2 loops of previous row, the joining loop and the next 2 loops, (cluster made), *net 7, net 5 together*, repeat.

Rows 12-14: ....plain.

Row 15: ....net 1, *work 9 knots in next loop, net 3*, repeat, ending with net 2 and a joining loop.

Rows 16-17: ....plain.

Row 18: ....net together without the mesh stick, last loop of previous row, the joining loop and the next 4 loops, (cluster made), *net 6, net 6 together*, repeat.

Rows 19–21:	plain.
Row 22:	net 1, *work 9 knots in next loop, net 6*, repeat, ending with net 5 and a joining loop.
Rows 23–25:	plain.
Row 26:	net 3, *net 9 together, net 6*, repeat, ending with net 2 and a joining loop.
Row 27:	*work 9 knots in next loop, net 6*, repeat, ending with net 5 and a joining loop.
Rows 28–30:	plain.
Row 31:	net 2, *net 9 together, net 6*, repeat, ending with net 3 and a joining loop.
Row 32:	(2.5 mm needle) plain.

Ripple mat

Finished size:	17 cm (6 ½ in) diameter
Equipment:	3 mm mesh stick (or knitting needle); 2 mm double-pointed knitting needle
Thread:	Gutermann quilting cotton 50; four blues, starting at centre with lightest blue and ending with darkest blue (colours 6217, 6126, 5624, 4932)

Row 1:	(3 mm mesh stick) cast on 10 loops (including the joining loop).
Row 2:	(2 mm needle) plain.

Change to 3 mm mesh stick for the rest of the mat, except for the last row.

Row 3:	4 knots in joining loop, *5 knots in each loop*, repeat to end of row.
Rows 4 & 5:	plain.
Row 6:	net 1, *net 5 together, net 5*, repeat, ending with net 3, and then a joining loop.
Row 7:	plain. Do not end with a joining loop but by netting alongside the 1st knot. Cut thread.
Row 8:	join in the next colour in the last loop of the previous row, leaving a tail for subsequent joining loops. Work another 9 knots in this loop, *net 2, 10 knots in next loop*, repeat, ending with net 2 and a joining loop.
Rows 9 & 10:	plain.
Row 11:	Net together without the mesh stick the last 2 loops of previous row, the joining loop and the next 2 loops (i.e. a cluster made without using the mesh stick), *net 7, net 5 together*, repeat, ending with net 7 and a joining loop.
Rows 12-14:	plain, finish as row 7.
Row 15:	join in the next colour in the last loop of the previous row, net 1, *8 knots in next loop, net 3*, repeat, ending with net 1 and a joining loop.
Rows 16-17:	plain.
Row 18:	net together without the mesh stick the last loop of previous row, the joining loop and the next 4 loops, *net 5, net 6 together*, repeat, ending with net 5 and a joining loop.
Rows 19-21:	plain, finish as row 7.
Row 22:	join in the next colour in the last loop of the previous row, net 1, *8 knots in next loop, net 2*, repeat. Omit net 2 at end of last repeat, and end with a joining loop.
Rows 23-24:	plain.
Row 25:	net together without the mesh stick the last loop of the previous row, the joining loop, and the next 5 loops, *net 3, net 7 together*, repeat, ending with net 3 and a joining loop.
Row 26:	(2 mm needle) net 1 without the needle, *net 2, net 2 together*, repeat, ending with net 3, working the last knot alongside the first knot.

This mat is worked from the same pattern as the ripple mat, but using a variegated thread (DMC tatting cotton) instead of changing colours, a 5 mm mesh stick and a 3 mm needle.

Rose stitch star mat

Finished size:	38 cm (14 3/4 in) diameter
Equipment:	2.5 mm and 3 mm double-pointed knitting needles; 6 mm, 8 mm and 10 mm mesh sticks
Thread:	DMC Cordonnet 60

Row 1: (8 mm mesh stick) cast on 16 loops (including joining loop).

Row 2: (2.5 mm needle) plain.

Row 3: (10 mm mesh stick) work 5 knots into joining loop, then *2 knots in first loop, 6 knots in next loop*, continue to end of row, ending with 2 knots in next loop and then a joining loop.

Row 4: (3 mm needle) net the first 2 loops together without using the needle, *net 1, join next 3 loops together*, repeat ending with net 1 and a joining loop [32 loops].

Rows 5 & 6: (3 mm needle) plain.

Row 7: (10 mm mesh stick) as row 3.

Row 8: (3 mm needle) as row 4 [64 loops].

Rows 9 & 10: (3 mm needle) plain.

Row 11: (10 mm mesh stick) 3 knots in joining loop, and then 4 knots in each loop.

Row 12: (10 mm mesh stick) *join 3 loops together, net 1*, repeat to end of row [128 loops].

Start of rose stitch star section

Row 13: (6 mm mesh stick) net 14, *7 knots in next loop, net 15*, omit net 15 at end of last repeat and finish with a joining loop.

Row 14: (2.5 mm needle) join last 3 loops in with joining loop, *work rose stitch in next 14 stitches, (join 4 loops together) twice*, omit 1 (join 4 loops together) at end of last repeat. (*Rose stitch*: draw the 1st loop up through the 2nd and net into it; draw the 2nd loop up through the 1st and net into it.)

Row 15: (6 mm mesh stick) 5 knots in joining loop, *4 knots in next loop, net 13, 4 knots in next loop, 6 knots in next loop*, omit 6 knots in next loop in last repeat.

Row 16: (2.5 mm needle) net 6, *join 4 loops, rose stitch next 12 loops, join 4 loops, net 7*, omit net 7 at end of last repeat.

Row 17: (6 mm mesh stick) net 7, *4 knots in next loop, net 11, 4 knots in next loop, net 8*, omit net 8 at end of last repeat.

Row 18:	(2.5 mm needle) net 8, *knot 4 loops together, rose stitch next 10 loops, join 4 loops, net 9*, omit net 9 at end of last repeat.
Row 19:	(6 mm mesh stick) net 9, *4 knots in next loop, net 9, 4 knots in next loop, net 10*, omit net 10 at end of last repeat.
Row 20:	(2.5 mm needle) net 10, *knot 4 loops together, rose stitch next 8 loops, join 4 loops, net 11*, omit net 11 at end of last repeat.
Row 21:	(6 mm mesh stick) net 11, *4 knots in next loop, net 7, 4 knots in next loop, net 12*, omit net 12 at end of last repeat.
Row 22:	(2.5 mm needle) net 12, *knot 4 loops together, rose stitch next 6 loops, join 4 loops, net 13*, omit net 13 at end of last repeat.
Row 23:	(6 mm mesh stick) net 13, *4 knots in next loop, net 5, 4 knots in next loop, net 14*, omit net 14 at end of last repeat.
Row 24:	(2.5 mm needle) net 14, *knot 4 loops together, rose stitch next 4 loops, join 4 loops, net 15*, omit net 15 at end of last repeat.
Row 25:	(6 mm mesh stick) net 15, *4 knots in next loop, net 3, 4 knots in next loop, net 16*, omit net 16 at end of last repeat.
Row 26:	(2.5 mm needle) net 16, *join 4 loops, rose stitch next 2 loops, join 4 loops, net 17*, omit net 17 at end of last repeat.
Row 27:	(6 mm mesh stick) net 17, *4 knots in next loop, net 1, 4 knots in next loop, net 18*, omit net 18 at end of last repeat.
Row 28:	(2.5 mm needle) net 18, *join 4 loops, join 4 loops, net 19*, omit net 19 at end of last repeat.
Row 29:	(6 mm mesh stick) net 19, *5 knots in next loop, net 20*, omit net 20 at end of last repeat.
Row 30:	(3 mm needle) net 20, *join 4 loops, net 21*, omit net 21 at end of last repeat.
Row 31:	(6 mm mesh stick) plain.
Row 32:	(3 mm needle) plain.
Row 33:	(10 mm mesh stick) *6 knots in next loop, net 1*, omit net 1 at end of last repeat.
Row 34:	(2.5 mm needle) *knot 3 loops together, net 1*, omit net 1 at end of last repeat.
Rows 35 & 36:	(2.5 mm needle) plain.
Row 37:	(10 mm mesh stick) plain.
Row 38:	(3 mm needle) net into the 1st loop without using the needle, and then join 2 loops together to end of row.

Stars

Christmas decorations can be made from netted stars. These can have either a looped edge or a straight edge.

 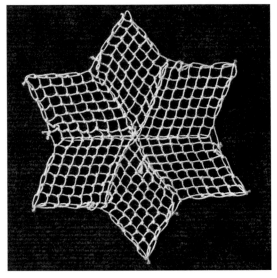

Star with looped edge and star with straight edge

Equipment: 3 mm double-pointed knitting needle
Thread: the first two stars were worked with Cebelia 30, and the gold star
                 with Cebelia 30 and a gold metallic thread (DMC art. 284) together.
                 The darning stitch embroidery around the edge was worked with
                 Twilley's Gold Dust 20.

Star with looped edge
Row 1:............Cast on 6 loops, including the joining loop.
Row 2:............2 knots in each loop.
Rows 3-7:............2 knots in each closed loop, 1 knot in the other loops.
Rows 8 & 9:............plain.

Points
Row 10:............net 6, turn.
Row 11:............net 5, turn.
Row 12:............net 4, turn.
Row 13:............net 3, turn.
Row 14:............net 2. Cut thread.

Join thread to the next loop of row 9, and work rows 10–14 again. Repeat around the rest of the star until you have 6 points.

Star with straight edge

Work rows 1–9 as above, then work as follows.

Join in the thread in a loop which is in line with the increase stitches in the body of the star.

Row 10: net 6, turn.

Row 11: net 4, net 2 together, turn.

Row 12: net 3, net 2 together, turn.

Row 13: net 2, net 2 together, turn.

Row 14: net 1, net 2 together, turn.

Row 15: join the last 2 loops together, without using the mesh stick.

Join thread to the next loop of row 9, and work rows 10–15 again. Repeat around the rest of the star until you have 6 points.

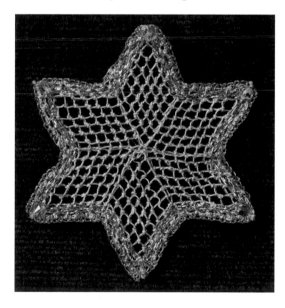

Straight-edged star, worked with metallic gold thread and decorated with beads and darning stitch outline.

Row 15: ....net 7, turn.

Row 16: ....net 6, turn.

Row 17: ....net 5, turn.

Row 18: ....net 4, turn.

Row 19: ....net 3, turn.

Row 20: ....net 2. Cut thread.

To work the other side of the oval, join the thread on the opposite side of the circle (see close-up photo) and repeat rows 4 to 20. You should now have 44 loops around the edge of the oval.

Close-up of centre of oval

Outer section

Row 21: ....(6 mm mesh stick) join thread to the right hand loop of the 2 loops at one end of the oval centre (make sure you leave a tail for making the joining loop in subsequent rows). Net 3 more knots into this loop and then continue as follows: 3 knots into the next 2 loops, net 16, 3 knots into the next 2 loops, 4 knots into next 2 loops, 3 knots into next 2 loops, net 16, 3 knots into next 2 loops, 4 knots into next loop. Finish with a joining loop [72 loops].

Row 22: ....(3 mm needle) plain.

Row 23: ....(2 mm needle) work 1 knot into the joining loop and then 2 knots in every loop [144 loops].

Rows 24–28: ....(2 mm needle) plain.

Row 29: ....(10 mm mesh stick) plain.

Row 30: ....(6 mm mesh stick) net the first 2 loops together without using the mesh stick (i.e. this joins the first 2 loops with the joining loop, forming a cluster), join 3 loops together to end of row [48 loops].

Row 31: ....(6 mm mesh stick) 1 knot into joining loop, 2 knots into next 9 loops, net 8, 2 knots into next 16 loops, net 8, 2 knots in to next 6 loops [80 loops].

Rows 32–37: ....(2 mm needle) work 1 knot into joining loop, *wrap thread once around needle and net into the next loop, net another knot into the same loop (loop stitch)*, repeat to end of row.

Row 38: .... (10 mm mesh stick) 2 knots in joining loop and then 3 knots into each long loop.

Rows 39–40: .... (2 mm needle) plain.

Row 41: .... (10 mm mesh stick) plain.

Row 42: .... (2 mm needle) gather the first 2 loops in with the joining loop, *wrap thread once around the needle, join 3 loops together*, repeat to end of row.

Shades of Blue mat

This mat is quite complicated so I have divided it up into sections. The first section, the centre section, is the most difficult part as it involves using two colours and is not worked in straightforward rows. The middle section is quite simple and is worked in normal rows. The last section is working the points. After the mat was completed I embroidered the points, as shown in the photograph, with DMC Pearl no. 8 using darning stitch.

Finished size: approximately 36 cm (14 in) diameter

Equipment: 6 mm and 8 mm mesh sticks; 2.5 mm double-pointed knitting needle

Thread: DMC crochet cotton no 40, light blue (800) and dark blue (799)

Section 1: Centre

Light blue

Cast on 16 loops (6 mm mesh stick). The rest of this section is worked with the 2.5 mm needle.

Light blue

Row 25: ....(8 mm mesh stick) plain.

Row 26: ....(2.5 mm needle) as row 24.

Section 3: Points

Dark blue (2.5 mm needle)

For the points the mat is divided up into eight lots of 24 loops.

Knot the thread into a loop of the previous row and work one plain row right around the mat (position the joining knot immediately above one of the outer leaves of the centre section.) After doing the joining loop turn work and net 23. Turn, net 22, turn. Continue in this way until you have completed the first point. Then work the other seven points. (See Chapter 4, page 38, for instructions on working a pointed edge with picots.)

· ·
The next four mats are embellished with linen stitch embroidery.
· ·

Octagonal mat

Finished size: approximately 40 cm (16 in) diameter

Equipment: 2.5 mm double-pointed knitting needle; 4 mm, 6 mm and 8 mm mesh sticks

Thread: Cebelia 30

For detailed instructions on working octagons see page 52.

Octagonal centre

(2.5 mm needle) cast on 20 loops.

Work 24 rows increasing at end of each row [44 loops].

Work 39 rows without increasing.

Work up the side for 19 loops. Cut thread.

Join in thread again at the bottom. Work one row plain [44 loops].

Decrease at beginning of each row until 19 loops remain.

Border

Join in a new thread (you can use this starting knot to join together the last 2 loops of the first row of the octagon), leaving a long tail for joining to subsequent rows.

Rows 1–4: (2.5 mm needle) plain, working 2 knots in each corner.

Row 5: (8 mm mesh stick) plain.

Row 6: (4 mm mesh stick) * join 2 loops together*.

Row 7: (8 mm mesh stick) 2 knots in each loop.

Rows 8–19: (2.5 mm needle) plain.

Row 20: (8 mm mesh stick) plain, working 2 knots in each corner.

Row 21: (6 mm mesh stick) *join 2 loops together*.

Row 22: (8 mm mesh stick) 2 knots in each loop.

Row 23: (4 mm mesh stick) plain, working 2 knots in each corner.

Row 24: (2.5 mm needle) plain, working 2 knots in each corner.

Row 25: (2.5 mm needle) plain.

Embroidery

Once the netting was completed I embroidered it in linen stitch with the same thread. See Appendix 1, page 133, for the pattern. I worked a single row of linen stitch around the outside edge.

Chequerboard mat

Finished size: approximately 16 cm (6 ¼ in) square, not including border

Equipment: 2 mm double-pointed knitting needle

Thread: DMC Special Dentelles, colours 754 and 3778, one ball of each

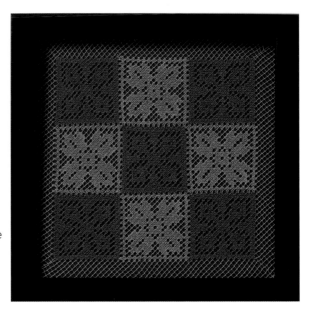

This mat uses two advanced techniques—working a square of diamond netting, and changing colours in the middle of the work (see Chapter 5 for instructions on working squares of diamond netting). Squares 1, 3, 5, 7 and 9 in one colour (I used dark pink). Squares 2, 4, 6 and 8 in contrasting colour (I used light pink).

Square 1 (dark pink)

Cast on 12 loops. Work using method 1 of instructions for square of diamond netting, but do not remove the foundation thread and do not knot the beginning and ending threads together. It is easier to do this knot once all the nine squares have been worked and the foundation thread removed.

1	2	3
4	5	6
7	8	9

Square 2 (light pink)

Place the foundation loop back on the pillow, but the opposite way to the way it was for the first square (i.e. the starting knot of the dark pink section will now be on the right hand side of the square). Cast on 12 loops on the foundation chain, but on the left side of the dark pink square. When you have finished the cast-on row, link your thread through the first dark pink loop. Do this at the end of every subsequent odd row. When you get to the end of the square, work up the side to the beginning, as you did for square 1.

Square 3 (dark pink)

Work as square 2, again casting on to the left of the first two squares.

Square 4 (light pink)

Knot into the 1st loop of the last row of square no 1 (i.e. at the left side edge). Net into each of the next 12 loops. Turn, and continue as for square 1. After working up the side, make your last knot alongside your 1st knot.

Square 5 (dark pink)

With square 4 to your right, knot into the 1st loop of the last row of square no 2 (the light pink square) and net into the next 12 light pink loops. Continue as for square 4, except that you link the thread through the light pink loops in alternate rows. Make your last knot alongside your first knot.

Square 6 (light pink)

With squares 4 and 5 to your right, knot into the first dark pink loop and work as square 5.

Square 7: ....(dark pink) work as square 4.

Square 8: ....(light pink) work as square 5.

Square 9: ....(dark pink) work as square 6.

When finished, remove foundation thread and complete the knots of the top row. Join the light pink thread to a loop on the outside edge and work 10 rows all around the edge, putting two knots in each corner. These extra rows are to assist with framing,

Blue and white mat

This piece was an experiment, to try out the idea of using two needles at the same time. To make the needles easier to manipulate, choose two needles of a similar size.

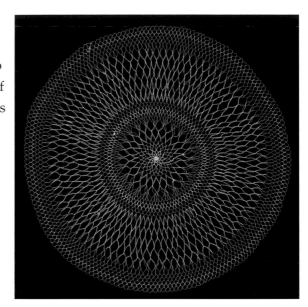

Finished size:	37 cm (13 ½ in) diameter
Equipment:	4 mm, 6 mm, 8 mm, 12 mm and 14 mm mesh sticks; 2.5 mm double-pointed knitting needles
Thread:	Crochet cotton no. 40, blue and white

Between rows 3 and 8 both blue and white tails are carried through the mat, so that either colour (or both) can be used. The white thread is cut off after row 8, and then joined in again at row 11. Rows 11–19 also have tails of both colours. If you prefer, the blue and white tails can be carried through the entire piece.

Wind two knitting needles with thread, one with blue and one with white.

Row 1: (4 mm mesh stick) white, cast on 12 loops.

Row 2: (2.5 mm needle) white, plain.

Row 3: (6 mm mesh stick) add in blue thread; using both needles together work a plain row. At end of row, do 2 joining loops, one for blue thread and one for white.

Row 4: (2.5 mm needle) blue. Before working this row, turn work and take the tail of the blue thread, thread it into a filet needle and work backward, making a knot into the white joining loop (this brings 3 threads together to make the tail for the next joining loop). Work 1 knot in every loop (i.e. both blue and white loops – this doubles the number of loops).

Row 5:	(4 mm mesh stick) white, plain.
Row 6:	(4 mm mesh stick) blue, plain.
Row 7:	(12 mm mesh stick) both needles, plain.
Row 8:	(12 mm mesh stick) both needles, plain. (Work a joining loop with the blue thread and finish off the white thread. Cut white thread).
Row 9:	(8 mm mesh stick) blue. Work another knot into the joining loop and then work 2 knots in every loop (both white and blue).
Row 10:	(4 mm mesh stick) blue, plain.
Rows 11 & 12:	(4 mm mesh stick) join in white thread again, plain.
Rows 13 & 14:	(4 mm mesh stick) blue, plain.
Rows 15-19:	(14 mm mesh stick) both needles, plain. End with a blue joining loop and finish off the white thread.
Row 20:	(8 mm mesh stick) blue, plain in every loop.
Rows 21-23:	(4 mm mesh stick) blue, plain.
Row 24:	(4 mm mesh stick) join in white thread again, plain. Finish off white thread and work a joining loop with the blue thread.
Row 25:	(4 mm mesh stick) blue, plain.
Row 26:	(2.5 mm needle) blue, plain.

Rings of Fire bag

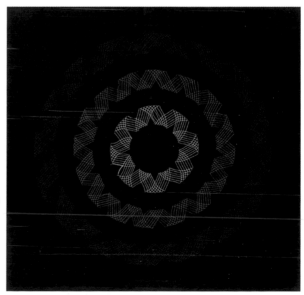

Finished size:	30 cm (12 in) diameter (size of lace)
Equipment:	1.5 mm and 3 mm double-pointed knitting needles; 18 mm and 20 mm mesh sticks
Thread:	Gutermann quilting cotton no. 50, four colours: black, yellow (688), orange (1576) and red (2074), or colours of your choice

Rectangular doily

Finished size:	4.3 x 3.2 cm (1 3/4 x 1 1/4 in)
Equipment:	1.25 mm, 1 mm and 0.75 mm double-pointed knitting needles
Thread:	Mettler embroidery cotton 60/2

Step 1: (0.75 mm needle) cast on 10 loops.

Step 2: (1 mm needle) Work 29 rows.

Step 3: remove foundation row and flip knots out. Work a row up the side back to the starting point. Work the last knot alongside the first knot. Cut thread.

Border

Join the thread to a loop on the edge, leaving a tail to use for the joining loops at the end of each row.

Row 1: (1.25 mm needle) work 2 knots in each loop, 4 in the corner loops.

Rows 2 & 3: (0.75 mm needle) work 1 knot in each loop.

Row 4: (1 mm needle) work 1 knot in every other loop.

See Appendix 1, page 122, for the embroidery pattern. Work it in linen stitch, using the same thread.

Oval doily

Finished size:	4 x 2.8 cm (1 1/2 x 1 1/8 in)
Equipment:	1.75 mm, 1.50 mm and 1.25 mm double-pointed knitting needles
Thread:	Mettler embroidery cotton 60/2

Row 1:	(1.50 mm needle) cast on 20 loops, including joining loop.
Rows 2–4:	(1.25 mm needle) plain.
Row 5:	(1.75 mm needle) *4 knots in each of the next 5 loops, net 5*, repeat.
Rows 6–8:	(1.25 mm needle) plain.
Row 9:	(1.75 mm needle) net into every second loop.

Remove the foundation loop and loosen the knots. Gather together 7 loops at one end (i.e. under the grouped knots) and knot them together. Using the same thread, join 3 sets of opposite loops to form the centre of the mat, and then gather together the 7 remaining loops at the other end and knot them together.

Octagonal mini doily

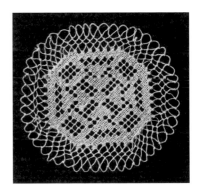

Finished size:	4 cm (1 1/2 in) diameter
Equipment:	0.75 mm, 1 mm and 1.50 mm double-pointed knitting needles
Thread:	Brok 100/3 for both net and linen stitch
Pattern:	7 meshes (sloping sides) x 8 meshes (straight sides)

With 0.75 mm needle, cast on 8 loops.

Change to 1 mm needle for the rest of the centre.

Increase at the end of the next 5 rows.

Work 15 rows plain.

Work up side for 7 loops.

Cut thread. Join in again at the bottom. Work one row plain.

Decrease at beginning of following rows until 7 loops are left.

Cut off the thread.

Working the border

Join in a new thread (you can use this starting knot to join together the last two loops of the first row of the octagon), leaving a long tail for joining to subsequent rows.

Tea cosy

Miniatures also lend themselves to a whimsical treatment. The tea cosy was made by working half of the miniature doily 3 to get a half circle, and a couple of rows were then added to the bottom. It was worked twice, and then the two halves joined together.

Miniature tables

The three miniature tables with accompanying lace could be placed in a doll's house, or in a display box as part of a miniature setting, or by themselves in a shadow box. Whichever way they are displayed they are sure to attract admiring comments.

Round table with tablecloth

Small table with doily

Oval table with doily

Filet patterns

Pattern sources

The first ten of these designs are taken from or adapted from patterns in antique sources, some of which are available in reproduction from Lacis Publications, 3163 Adeline Street, Berkeley, CA 94703; www.lacis.com. Lacis also stock tools for netting.

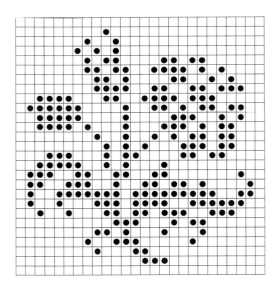 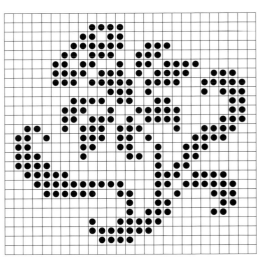

Left: Small flower, *Grand Album de Modèles pour Filet no 7*, page 19.
Right: Daffodil, *Grand Album de Modèles pour Filet No 7*, page 19.

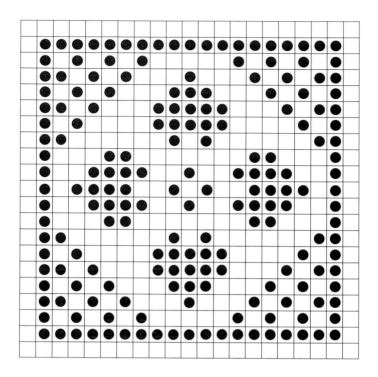

Pattern for miniature cushion, Margaret Morgan.

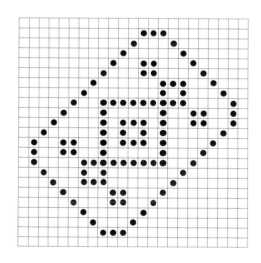

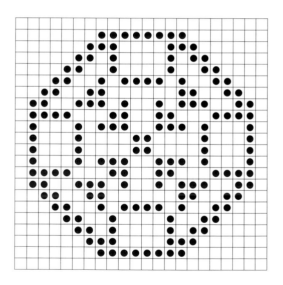

Left: Pattern for miniature rectangular doily, Margaret Morgan.

Right: Pattern for miniature octagon, Margaret Morgan.

APPENDIX 2
Glossary of terms

Closed loop: a loop which begins and ends in a single loop of the preceding round – that is, the two knots which form the loop are made in the same loop of the preceding round.

Foundation chain: a long strip of netting, usually two stitches wide, which is used in place of a foundation loop. It is usually cut away when the piece is finished.

Foundation loop: a length of thread with the two ends knotted together to form a circle. The first knots of a piece of netting are made onto the foundation loop.

Joining loop: the loop at the end of each round in circular netting. The loop is made by knotting together the working thread and the long tail which travels from the centre of the circle to the outside edge.

Left and right
long loops: the loops used in Swiss diamond netting, which are longer than, and to the right and left of, a series of shorter loops.

Working thread: the thread which comes from the netting needle.

Index of stitches

Bibliography

There are not many books specifically on netting, and the few that have been published in the past are mostly now out of print. A good source of information and patterns are old magazines, such as Weldon's magazines. Fortunately, some of these have been republished in book form in recent years.

The following is a list of books which have at least sections on netting. Although some of them are out of print, they occasionally become available from second-hand shops or suppliers.

Encyclopaedias

De Dillmont, Thérèse. *The Complete DMC Encyclopedia of Needlework*, Running Press, Philadelphia, PA, 1978.

Weldons Encyclopedia of Needlework, London, n.d.

Nuova Enciclopedia dei Lavori Femminili, Mani di Fata, Milan, 1991.

Other books and magazines

Kliot, Jules & Kaethe (eds). *The Art of Netting*, Lacis, Berkeley, CA, 1989.

Kliot, Jules & Kaethe (eds). *Netting from Early Sources*, Lacis, Berkeley, CA, 1998.

Knight, Pauline. *The Technique of Filet Lace*, Batsford, London, 1980.

Leszner, Eva María (ed.) *Netznadel arbeiten: filetknoten und sticken*, Rosenheimer Verlagshaus, Rosenheim, Germany, 1983.

Mani di Fata (magazine). *La rete a rosoni*, Milangrafica, Milan, 1981.

Melen, Lisa. *Knotting & Netting, the Art of Filet Work*, Van Nostrand Reinhold, New York and London, 1972.

Mussalo, Ella & Avelin, Liisa, *Kymijokilaakson verkkopitsit*, Kotka, Finland, 1986.

Strub, Maria. *Filetknüpfen/Filet noué*, Lang & Cie, Reiden, Switzerland, n.d.